Praise

Everybody has childhood memories of growing up with friends and neighbors who are unforgettable. Vic Wilson grew up in the 1960s in a mill village, New Holland, just outside Gainesville, Georgia. In their own tight-knit community, the youngsters found entertainment around every corner, whether it be sneaking into the mill recreation center or playing creative games in the yards and streets. Vic was a "MilliKid," so named for the children of workers at the Milliken textile mill. In his book, he captures these adventures in an entertaining, story-telling way that will resonate with anyone who lived in such a close neighborhood.

– Johnny Vardeman

MilliKids

Cheryl,
Cheerful Memories,
May God bless,
Vic Wilson

MilliKids

It Took a Mill to Raise a Village

Vic Wilson

BOOKLOGIX®
Alpharetta, Georgia

Copyright © 2012 by Vic Wilson

All rights reserved. No part of this book may be reproduced or transmitted in any form or by any means, electronic or mechanical, including photocopying, recording, or any information storage and retrieval system, without permission in writing from Vic Wilson.

ISBN: 978-1-61005-299-3

Library of Congress Control Number: 2012923196

Printed in the United States of America

∞ This paper meets the requirements of ANSI/NISO Z39.48-1992 (Permanence of Paper)

The author has tried to recreate events, locations, and conversations from his/her memories of them. In some instances, in order to maintain their anonymity, the author has changed the names of individuals and places. He/she may also have changed some identifying characteristics and details such as physical attributes, occupations, and places of residence.

This book is dedicated to my wife Joan and my grandson, Jackson Lee. Jackson is a life changer and one of the greatest joys of my life. His insistence on my telling him these stories led to me writing them.

"...all things..."

– Romans 8:28

New Holland is not just where I am from, it is who I am.

– Vic Wilson

Contents

Foreword	xi
Acknowledgments	xiii
Introduction	xv
Chapter 1 Miss Icie	1
Chapter 2 Hunky Wagon	9
Chapter 3 Wicket Wizards	17
Chapter 4 Pilgrim's Café	23
Chapter 5 Pasture Surfing	29
Chapter 6 Goodbye Is Never Easy	35
Chapter 7 Little Dink's Fall	41
Chapter 8 Gillespie's Bus	47
Chapter 9 Big Dink's Peppers	53
Chapter 10 Never Enough	59
Chapter 11 Mr. Pete and Mr. Manley	65
Chapter 12 Shattered Dream	73
Chapter 13 Dead Man's Curve	81
Chapter 14 Wheels	89
Chapter 15 Listen and Learn	97
Chapter 16 Waterless Chasm	105
Chapter 17 Crocker Gator	111
Chapter 18 Shock and Riles	119
Chapter 19 W & W Bike Repair	127
Chapter 20 Bible School Blues	135
Chapter 21 Joyful Noise Janitor	143
Chapter 22 Carolina Crash	151

Chapter 23 Suislide on Spring	157
Chapter 24 MilliKat	165
Chapter 25 Witch Hazel	171
Chapter 26 Saved by the Church Steps	177
Chapter 27 Emo's World	185
Chapter 28 Skinny Dip	193
Chapter 29 The Fire	199

Foreword

Victor Wilson and I have a history. As an elementary student at New Holland School, I knew Vic as my classmate Garry's baby brother. As a parent of a sixth grade son, I renewed my friendship with Vic through his wife Joan, my son's teacher. Later, as my family matured, I returned to teaching and Mr. Wilson served as my assistant principal at North Hall Middle School. My advice to young people is to be conscious of your behavior at all times, because people re-enter your life at strange times and in different positions.

New Holland Mill Village was the place that probably shaped both our lives the most. It is where we grew up and developed, with the influences of school, church, and community. I am delighted that Vic is sharing his memories of growing up among the wonderful people who impacted and helped mold us into the people we have become.

Sandra Dunagan Deal
First Lady of Georgia
November 20, 2012

Acknowledgments

Words cannot adequately express my love and appreciation for my wife, Joan. She has been encouraging me for forty years and none of this is possible without her.

I would also like to thank my sister, Merla. She has always believed in me and told me so.

Many thanks to the publishing staff at BookLogix, Anne Davenport of Matthews Printing, and Johnny Vardeman.

Introduction

New Holland

It Took a Mill to Raise a Village

More than 650,000 men died in what was called a Civil War. The War Between the States (1861–1865) ripped a gaping wound in our country, and in every community from Texas to Maine. It divided households and tore families apart. Brothers fought against brothers and in some instances, fathers against sons. How can a nation recover from such calamity? Where does the greatest country in the world begin rebuilding? How many ancestral lines ended as a result of this war?

It has often been said that "it takes a village to raise a child." Nestled on 560 acres of rolling terrain blessed by a warm and revitalizing stream called Limestone Springs, lies a small village affectionately and proudly called New Holland. This post-Civil War and Industrialized Southern village would not have known life if it weren't for this horrendous bloodshed. Centered in this village is the

Milliken Cotton Mill. At its inception in the 1890s, the mill and its hundreds of duplex houses were built by the Pacolet Manufacturing Company—the forerunner of Milliken.

A Southern gentleman, Captain John H. Montgomery, and a Northern aristocrat, Seth Milliken, happened to share a simple dream—bringing jobs, industry, and a new beginning to a tiny North Georgia town called New Holland. The country's spirit was broken, people were out of work, and a new industrial birth pang was rumbling from coast to coast. Cotton was abundant, and Captain Montgomery and Mr. Milliken vowed to each other, and to God, to make a difference by offering people hope and a chance to ease the pain and suffering of the past.

Original planning called for the mill to be the center of the village, where its one main road would gracefully weave its way around the mill leading to the nearby township, Gainesville, two miles away. However, local politicians and company officials reluctantly decided to build the mill on the south side of the main road. The railroad company would then have easy access to deliver railway cars with bales of cotton to the rear of the mill. Several beautifully landscaped streets were constructed on the opposite side of the road leading up the gentle hills and sloping terraces. There the mill's owners would build houses to rent its workers. Word quickly spread, and families from Tennessee, North and South Carolina, and other parts of Georgia raced in covered wagons and on horseback to find work and, hopefully, a new home. It was a great opportunity for a new start.

As travelers descended into the village on the road running east and west, they were struck by the awesome sight of a five-story brick cotton mill on one side of the road with a towering water tank that fed the village gracefully adorning the top of a hill on the other side. These travelers and visitors had to cross Limestone Springs, known for its "healing waters." Limestone Springs, or New Holland Springs Resort, was built to attract visitors and vacationers.

The policy of the mill—made possible by the Montgomery family, who are considered part of the founding members of New Holland—was to provide all employees comfortable homes, good schools and churches, enriching recreational activities, a clean environment, and an opportunity to earn and save. Captain Montgomery developed this policy, which came from his personal vision of generosity and an unfailing obligation to God.

The mill suffered damage by a tornado in 1903, but was brought to repair and restoration by Mr. S. (Seth) M. Milliken who, and without delay, came to the rescue of the Pacolet Company, and more importantly, the citizens that worked and lived in the New Holland village. Mr. Milliken, the grandfather of Roger Milliken, who led the company for seventy-one years (and who passed away on Dec. 30, 2010), was approached by Captain Montgomery for assistance. Before the Captain could complete his request, Mr. Milliken informed him that in order for restoration to occur all Captain Montgomery had to do was ask, at which time the money and any other needs would be met for the resurrection of the village. Captain Montgomery responded immediately.

The mill was restored, the village repaired, and the people realized that together anything could be accomplished. Pacolet and Milliken eventually rebuilt homes, a church, a school, a clinic, an auditorium, a complete gymnasium, and stores that made New Holland a self-sustaining model mill village. This spirit of resurgence and hope continues to pervade the village of New Holland and its patriots even today. While many changes occurred in the business world, while the economy continued to tank, and while different cultures ventured into the mill community, these were not things these brave and resilient people had not overcome and put behind them before.

Through the tornado of 1903, World War I, the Great Depression, the tornado of 1936, World War II, the Korean War, the Vietnam War, and all other events that presented themselves to cause a people to give up and give in, New Holland reigned tall and proud. It has lost some of its brave citizens to all the wars, the economic woes, and the tornadoes, but New Holland never folded, gave up, or gave in. It only grew tighter and became more determined than ever as a small cotton mill community.

The "MilliKids" evolved from being recipients of what Captain Montgomery and Roger Milliken created, a village where a cotton mill provided everything.

It could have been just MillKids, but an "i" was added to honor the Milliken family. We romped, ran, biked, skated, and skipped up and down the streets, sidewalks, and backyards of New Holland knowing we were looked after by many adults — not just our own parents, but others who felt an urgent responsibility to teach and protect every child. We knew we were safe, but most importantly we felt loved — an abiding love that still exists throughout our small community and even into our extended families today.

My name is Will, and I am very proud to have been raised a "MilliKid." These are stories about a few of us. We each had our own problems, but look back with a smile and thank God we lived in a community where people really cared. Each story is how I remember it. The cast of MilliKids may not have been the exact characters in each case, but the theme remains the same. In some cases, the stories have been changed enough to avoid possible humiliation and harm to anyone. Several of these stories might have happened a little differently, but changes were made to appeal to the reader.

I am a very fortunate and most blessed person to have had the greatest childhood ever — better than Mayberry even — but more importantly, to be surrounded with the finest family and a cast of friends that causes me to look back with gratitude and appreciation for their impact on my life. They were instrumental in making me who I am today. We laughed, we cried, we fussed, and had a wonderful time doing so.

A good memory allows one to relive his life, especially if it is filled with joyful and meaningful stories. I would like to share a few with you.

Chapter 1
Miss Icie

Growing up in a mill village was fun and safe. Usually the cotton mill provided most everything needed to have a happy childhood: a gym, ball field, school, clinic, churches, stores, firehouse, and employment for parents by the Milliken Company, which owned and operated the mill. No guarantees, mind you, but we had it all, so it seemed. We didn't know any better; we were just kids, MilliKids.

Will, that's me, was the leader of the pack, being the oldest at twelve, tallest, and most athletic, so I thought. My life was centered on basketball, baseball and my friends. I was thin, timid, and scared of girls. One of my strengths was the ability to convince one of my younger friends to do things I wasn't quite willing or brave enough to do myself.

Little Dink was the fighter. Even at eight years of age he didn't let anyone push him or his friends around. He was somewhat stocky, let's say chubby, but he didn't take any guff off anybody. He liked being bullied because he didn't know any better than to call the bully's bluff. He was younger but he acted older.

Stump was nine, somewhat athletic, but more musically inclined. He was willing to do most anything as long as he had an audience. His nickname came as he sat on an old tree stump one day filled with hornets. Enough said! He was above average in weight and height and always seemed to have his mouth open, for whatever reason.

Wart was eight and a constant nuisance, hence, Wart. He was spoiled and smaller than the rest of us. Being the only child and having parents that thought he could do no wrong, we had to look after him the most. He was one of us, and we let him be himself. He knew how to push everyone's buttons, and we spent most of the summers in this little mill village keeping him out of trouble. We were buddies and we had a ball. Too bad we had to grow up…almost.

Most of our summer days were either spent on the croquet court located behind the gym, on the basketball court in the gym, playing hide-and-go-seek and fox-and-hounds, or on the baseball field behind our elementary school. In the pasture, we often slipped and slid down the tall grass hills on cardboard. Many days, especially when it rained, we played Monopoly on one of our front porches or went to visit our most faithful ally, Miss Icie.

Miss Icie loved to see us. Often she would cook divinity, a Southern candy, or chocolate fudge just for us. She always greeted us with a smile and something warm to say. We knew we were safe around her. She was a nurse until nature interfered, and in a horrible way.

"There's my boys! What on earth can you guys be up to today?" she would say when we caught her eye. Her voice was smooth and melodic. She was a paraplegic. Polio had robbed her of the joys we experienced, and I guess she lived through us; actually, she was one of us. We knew this kind, old saint of a lady in her wheelchair prayed for us each day because she loved us; she loved everyone. Her smile still follows me. I believe she was an angel sent from heaven above to look over us and provide a safe and warm second home. In my mind I can still see her on her front porch in her wheelchair, with the widest smile on her face.

"Now, go on in the house and help yourself to some fresh chocolate fudge. I made it just for you boys," she would say.

Can you imagine going into someone's home today to help yourself? She trusted us, and we felt it. We did indeed help ourselves to her goodies.

Little Dink and Stump wanted to camp out behind Miss Icie's house one night. Daddy had an old, mossy green tarp that we used as our tent. It didn't have pegs and stakes like most tents. We used broomsticks and cement blocks to hold it up and in place. It always smelled rotten, and I'm sure that it not being cleaned in more than forty years contributed to that distinct odor.

"Will, you got the tent ready? It might rain tonight. Are there many holes? Make sure I sleep on the other side where it's dry," Little Dink insisted.

Sometimes there were more than just the four of us all warm and cozy in the tent. In order to camp out we had to have some snacks and drinks to make it complete. We would all gather together what coins we could scrape up. We had collected just enough money for maybe one of us to enjoy a soft drink, chips, or candy bar. However, we constantly looked out for each other and wouldn't dare venture to the store without enough money for one and all.

"Twenty-seven cents won't buy much today," Wart blurted. "I'll tell you what; I know where Mama keeps her change purse. Let me see what I can get without her missing it."

Usually, we wouldn't even think of Wart or anyone else in our crew attempting to do something we knew would upset our parents, but we were desperate. We didn't encourage or discourage; we let Wart take full responsibility for the results.

A few seconds after he left our sight, Wart ran back across his backyard with what we thought would put us over the top. Not this time.

He ran for his life, shouting "Run, run, run, they caught me, I got nothing!"

The three of us took off, we didn't know why. We were innocent, but there was enough guilt for other things we shouldn't have done to go around. We still had a dilemma, not enough money for tonight's goodies. To ask our parents for the extra cash never crossed our minds, because we already knew the answer, so we scattered.

I delivered papers and mowed lawns for several neighbors so I had enough change to get us started in our efforts to buy what we needed. We gathered empty Coke bottles — glass ones of course, no plastic yet — and took them to Kroger's, where we knew the manager, Mr. McDonald, would give us at least three cents for each empty bottle. He preferred Coca-Cola bottles but we would slip in an occasional Pepsi, RC, or Dr. Pepper. I often dreamed that I would bag groceries for him one day. Anyway, today we were short of our goal. We had already scoured the neighborhood for empties, we even begged, but we still needed several more bottles.

The four of us regrouped and wound up on Miss Icie's porch, where we sat, heavy with breath, and nervous laughter. Nervous, because we still expected Wart's mom or dad, usually his dad, to come around the end of the porch looking for us.

Noticing our bitter disappointment from our failed efforts caught Miss Icie's attention.

"What's going on, guys?" Miss Icie asked.

Before I could set the stage with a lame excuse, Little Dink had to squeal, "Wart almost got us into trouble with his parents.

In his search for extra change for our campout, his parents walked in on him."

When Miss Icie heard this, she told us she believed she had some empties in her crawlspace under her house. Everyone drank Cokes, even Miss Icie. Most of the families weren't fortunate enough in the mill village to have a basement. The floors were typically old red clay/dirt, full of childhood memories and sometimes (miraculously) dirty, empty bottles. We discovered she had crates of bottles. It was like a treasure chest of possibilities right there under our noses. If we had known about yard sales…well, you get the picture.

One thing about MilliKids, that's truer today for those of us that hold on to those memories, is that we did not take advantage of other people's possessions. We took what we thought was alright to take, enough bottles for this campout.

Miss Jessup, another neighbor who lived next door to Miss Icie, often took us places when no other parents could. Miss Jessup had this old '57 Chevy station wagon, mean, rusty, and green (an old ugly green). She loaded us up, bottles and all, and headed off for Kroger's. She usually needed something from the store anyway.

Mr. McDonald, the manager of Kroger, appeared like he expected us. When we pulled up in front of the store he had a couple of his bag boys rush out to help us unload and quicken our search for the goodies we needed for the campout. He made sure even after he asked us how many bottles we had, to give us a few more coins than we deserved. He looked like he knew what we were up to.

We loaded up chips, drinks, candy—more than we needed, but we knew why we bought extra stuff. Back in the old station wagon, we found ourselves excited about the night to come. Two miles later, with one big, brown grocery bag full of treats, we pulled up on Spring Street to begin our night to remember. The extra stuff? Miss Icie had a sweet tooth—we knew it, and it made us feel safe to sleep in her backyard and eat treats made possible by her generosity. We gave Miss Icie reason to smile. You see, *others matter*, especially Miss Icie.

Chapter 2
Hunky Wagon

I don't know of a child today that doesn't have enough change for a snack or drink out of one of the many vending machines strategically placed everywhere. Whether at school or the mall, there are machines with just about anything for anybody. People can afford things today that we MilliKids could not afford. Once in a while, when the Hunky Wagon made its daily trips up and down the streets of the village, we became extremely resourceful at securing a nickel or dime for the ice cream treats the wagon brought into the neighborhood each day.

When we could scrounge together the change, the Hunky Wagon, as we called it (I have no idea how it got its name), was a wonderful sight. The wagon was a paneled truck that had been converted into a refrigerated blessing of frozen delights. The truck was covered with stickers advertising all the different ice creams and popsicles that were available.

The truck had this melodious tone so recognizable that we could hear it five village blocks away. The sound was an early warning signal to us kids to try and find a coin for a frozen delicacy. The MilliKids were no different from most others except we didn't carry change ordinarily, because we didn't have any. So you can imagine the promises we made to our mothers if only they would give us a nickel or two. The more money you had, the bigger the ice cream and the opportunity to share with a friend who didn't have any money, and this happened quite often.

Mama always kept a few coins in a Mason jar on a shelf just inside the downstairs closet, right above the top of the door. Everyone in the house knew where this jar was, but we also knew better than to take even one penny without permission. If she felt pity for me or my friends, she would nod her head, and I knew that meant I could run to that jar and get just enough nickels for whatever friends were at my house. She didn't always nod her head, and I never pushed her on it. I knew she had good reason to not allow us this occasional pleasure, later I would accept and understand why.

For some reason that I have never really understood, Little Dink and Wart always had coins while Stump and I didn't. We shared just about everything, but once in a while we had to watch those two enjoy their tasty fudge bars,

Creamsicles, or hunkies (vanilla ice cream covered in chocolate on a stick). We imagined the cold, creamy, flavorful, and terribly sweet treat finding its way down their throats and into their bloated bellies. I closed my eyes and began licking my lips, trying to imagine the cool, refreshing treat easing its way into…no good. We also realized that tomorrow was another day and time to create ideas to avoid feeling left out again.

I remember one such day, Stump and I were sitting on the ground while Little Dink and Wart enjoyed their Hunky Wagon treats.

"You wouldn't believe how good this Creamsicle is today," Little Dink blurted. "I wish you could have some, but that would mean less for me, hahahaha."

"Yep, what a treat. I'm gonna save this extra dime so I can have two of these tomorrow," Wart remarked, slurping a Creamsicle of his own.

"Wart, I've had just about enough of you, you little runt," Stump barked as he started chasing Wart.

Between his laughs and licks, Wart stumbled on the sidewalk curb and sprawled onto Spring Street. The Creamsicle smeared in the middle of the road.

Everyone started to laugh except Wart — he was furious. "I'm going to tell my mama and daddy on you," Wart shot back as he darted off to his house.

"That was better than the ice cream," I said.

We three sat there and laughed hysterically for several minutes before it occurred to us that maybe his daddy would show up to chew on us.

"What will we do if his daddy shows up?" Stump asked.

"He won't. He's at work in the mill, we're fine," I said.

Wart's dad worked the first shift in the cotton mill and didn't get off until four o'clock. It was close, but I knew it wasn't time yet. We weren't worried about Wart's mama; she was a kind woman and wouldn't say one thing to us. Knowing her, she would probably give Wart a dollar just to shut him up.

We could still hear the Hunky Wagon as it wound its way down and around Spring Street, and onto Victor Street. When the truck reached the highway at the bottom of the hill it would turn left, venture over to East Main Street, dispense what goodies it could before it got to the top, and turned around to return toward the Gainesville (Gainesville was the county hub) end of the village. We never knew or even wondered where that wagon began or ended its' day, but we always saw it at the bottom of Spring Street as it returned to its mysterious origin.

"Boy, was that good," Little Dink said as he finished with two or three final licks of his stick.

"All right, enough is enough," I said as we moved over to the church steps where we often gathered during the day.

We didn't congregate there on Sunday, just all the other times when no one was inside. We glanced down at the bottom of Spring Street and, wouldn't you know it, there was Wart and his mama. They flagged the wagon down so he could have another ice cream. We just looked at each other and shook our heads in amazement.

Little Dink, Stump, and I continued to sit there on the church steps until we could no longer hear the distinct sound that came from the lone speaker on top of the Hunky Wagon. It was gone, and so were our hopes to get an ice cream this day, but wait...

"I've got an idea," Stump said, turning to Little Dink and me. "Don't you remember, Wart said he had a dime to buy two treats tomorrow. Now our job is to get that dime from him, but how?"

We started plotting ways to con the coin away from the brat. We looked at each other, and I could tell Stump had an idea.

"Okay, guys, we've got to pretend we have something of value, but will not share it with Wart." Stump began. "You know how nosy he is, he's got to have it, especially if it seems important to us."

Wart was a couple of years younger and somewhat smaller so we were able to talk him into things to make him feel like he belonged. We came up with a brilliant idea — all for one measly ten-cent piece.

The next day, a couple of hours before we knew the Hunky Wagon would arrive, we arranged to play baseball, and, yes, Wart had returned like nothing had ever happened. This was not the first time for one of our plots, so we didn't bring up the incident from the day before and neither did he.

"Did you guys hear that the Hunky Wagon will not be around today?" Stump asked. "Something's wrong with the transmission. Anyway, it's about time to get some more of Mr. Cody's apples, what do you say?"

Mr. Cody lived several blocks away, and one of our summertime "sneak-and-take" plans was to visit his apple tree after sunset. We'd make sure his house was dark and make our way up the tree and have off with some of his juicy apples.

"Sounds like a great idea to me," I responded. "Only this time Wart will have to climb the tree and get his own."

Wart was not only afraid to climb Mr. Cody's apple tree but he was also afraid of the dark.

"Come on, guys, you know I can't climb that tree and besides, you usually bring me back a couple of apples anyway." Wart said.

"Well, what do you have for a few apples?" I asked.

That's right, a few apples for one thin dime. We had our coin and today's mission was almost a success.

"You'll have to pay us now," Stump demanded.

Wart pulled the dime out of his pocket and gave it to me. He had no sooner turned the dime loose, when the most beautiful music in the world at 3:15 p.m. on a hot summer afternoon began to fill the village.

"I guess they fixed the transmission," Stump barked with a laugh.

Little Dink looked at me, I looked at Stump, and we choked back tears of joy just in time.

Needless to say, we had the best popsicles in the world that afternoon. We never let on, and, yes, Wart got his apples not knowing any better.

We decided to get popsicles because they came with double sticks for frozen fun, and for another reason—Wart didn't have any money. Yes, we shared.

Chapter 3

Wicket Wizards

MilliKids were competitive. It didn't matter what the sport or subject was, we were always trying to outdo each other. Sometimes it became a little too physical with the pushes, shoves, and just being mean to each other in order to get our way, but in the end we wound up friends—quick to forgive and forget the other's misgivings.

As a child in a textile mill village, there were always old people. Now, when I say old people, what I really mean is a bunch of men and women who in their 40s and 50s looked old, gray, and wrinkly, but for good reason—the mill. It wasn't that the mill was unsanitary or unsafe, it was just plain hard work. Eight-hour shifts with lint filled lungs and eyes.

The New Holland Gym provided a break from their routine of millwork. It offered and maintained bowling leagues, called ten pins, with its two alleys in its lowest level. It was the home to an indoor, steam-heated swimming pool, and the floor just above it was the basketball court.

The village was complete. It offered not only what the gym provided in the form of entertainment and exercise, but it also maintained a baseball field, which served as a playground for New Holland Elementary School's first through eighth grades. Besides all this, we had shuffleboard pads, horseshoe boxes, and our very own croquet court.

Croquet was part of our culture and offered daily relaxation and exercise for our older gentlemen. The men would gather at the packed sand and red clay court every day in the early morning, choose teams, and spend hours on the croquet court before they left for work at the mill, or just went home. Occasionally, other men would get off work and quickly retreat to the court.

It was usually me, Little Dink, and Stump who raced to the court every morning and hoped that we would get called on to run an errand and buy the players a Coke and bag of peanuts from Miss Bee's Beauty Shop across the way. Whoever went usually got a free Coke and bag of peanuts and quickly returned to watch the fun and excitement of a croquet game between these old men.

You could expect to see the regulars: Newt from East Main Street, Wormy from Carolina Street, Coot from Spring Street, and Ole Man Delong. We still have no clue where he lived. It didn't matter — they all lived on the court, more or less.

As the oldest of the MilliKids, if one of the older men was running late or didn't show, I was asked to play on one of the teams until a regular arrived.

The true ages of these men weren't known, but they did appear ancient and worn. At least until teams were drawn and wickets inserted into the clay, then suddenly, they became little boys once again. Croquet and competition were like a drug. The wickets, balls, and mallets were kept under lock and key in a galvanized box, about two feet by two feet by one foot deep, mounted to a light pole at one end of the croquet court. Later on, it became a summer chore, rather a joyful responsibility, for me to unlock and set up the wickets before the men arrived each morning.

"Okay Coot, you and I are the captains today," Newt barked. "Let's flip a coin to see who chooses first."

"Me and Delong are gonna be partners today." Coot quipped.

"Not so fast, Coot, what makes you think I wanna be on your team," Ole Man Delong snapped back.

"Heads or tails, Coot," Newt insisted.

"All right, all right, tails," Coot shot back.

Without even looking at the coin, "It's heads, me and Delong, and that settles that," snapped Newt.

"Let me see the coin, Newt," Coot angrily snorted.

It didn't do any good—it never did, this was the way teams were chosen. Anyway, they always changed partners after the first game.

The three of us always sat on the bench near the croquet box at the end of the court to anxiously await our opportunity to head off to Miss Bee's for their snack. Every now and then, a neighbor would bring his lawn chair and enjoy the festivities. He would unfold it and usually sit at the top of the hill. Many sat on the ground, backs against the old oak tree overlooking the court, to enjoy the verbal exchanges that occurred at every game. The players usually took a couple of breaks during the morning, right up until dinner time when they would head home, eat, return, and start the shenanigans all over again.

This particular Friday morning, I was a little late getting to the court. Stump would be the first to provide the refreshments, then Little Dink, and then me. Sometimes it never made it to the third kid on the bench, and that was all right too. We always shared. I wouldn't dare do it today, but we didn't think twice about drinking out of the same bottle. It was cold, it was delicious, and it was a treat most of us weren't allowed to enjoy at home.

Stump returned from Miss Bee's somewhat slower than usual. It didn't take us long to figure out why. By the time he got to the top of the hill on the far end of the court, we could tell he already had his share of Coke. It was exceptionally hot that day and Stump was making us hotter.

Wicket Wizards

Little Dink took off, knocked the bench over with me still on it and ran to get a sip. I really didn't care. I picked myself up, straightened the bench and took my seat again. Something more important was on my mind.

Newt and Ole Man Delong won the first match handily. Newt was also quick to notice that I didn't get any of the drink. He came over, placed his hand on my shoulder, handed me a nickel, and said, "I saw what those boys were up to Will. Go get yourself a Coke on me."

I had never seen this side of Newt. We were usually just runt kids in his eyes. He could tell something was not quite the same. Maybe he had already heard, maybe he knew. It was difficult to keep something quiet for long in a small neighborhood such as ours.

I wanted to take the nickel, go to Miss Bee's, get myself a Coke and drink it in front of them, but I couldn't. I wasn't thirsty, so I kindly declined Newt's offer. Oh, by the way, MilliKids were always kind and respectful. "Yes, ma'am" and "no, sir" was the way we talked; it was how we were raised.

"No sir, I appreciate it, but I'm not thirsty," I said.

"Keep it boy; you'll get thirsty soon enough." Newt remarked.

"Thank you, sir," I said.

Stump and Little Dink didn't know what had happened, and I never told them. I also never told them the reason I was late that morning. Even though it was sunny and in the nineties, this day remained cloudy and gray because of the news I received right before I came to the croquet court.

It was early, probably around eight o'clock in the morning and my aunt, my mother's sister, was at our house. I didn't know why, and I didn't ask questions. I don't recall all the details except my mama was going into the hospital for breast cancer surgery.

My aunt, in her harsh tone, said, "Your mama's got cancer. It's serious, and she may not be around much longer."

What was I to do? I didn't even know what cancer was, breast or any other kind. But I knew from my aunt's voice that it wasn't good, and that I may not have my mother much longer. She was my best friend.

My mother lived for twenty-one years after this diagnosis and operation, and even a subsequent cancer operation. Hers was not a full and healthy life, but she lived for many more years. I have always believed that her fire and determination defeated death. She also had a strong desire to be around her children and grandchildren for as long as she was able. I will never forget that horrific feeling that ran through me when I heard the words, "she may not be around much longer."

The croquet court was always a sanctuary for me, but not this day. However, the offer of a nickel from Newt helped make it a little better. I never got to thank him, but I will never forget him. Not because of a coin, not that it would probably be used to satisfy a thirst or a sweet tooth, but that it came at a time when I needed to see a kind face, hear a good word, and feel like someone, even someone that hardly knew me, actually cared.

Chapter 4
Pilgrim's Café

The summer heat was brutal. On this weekday afternoon, it was so hot and humid you could see the zigzag of the heat rays swirling above the street. Even the MilliKids couldn't invent ways to have fun. Usually, we would gather on one of our front porches and play Monopoly. Not today; it was unbearable. We tried to get a game started at Little Dink's, but decided to go home and wait until the cooler part of the evening arrived, hopefully.

It was a little past dinner. Dinner time in the South is like lunch to the rest of the world. Anyway, it was around one o'clock and cotton mill hands, otherwise known as lintheads, were eating lunch before returning to work. You could often see the workers spread out on the ledges of the raised windows in the mill during dinner break. They were on the ledges because the air-conditioned system had not been installed in the mill yet. At the end of Spring Street next to the mill was Pilgrim's Café. Most of the lintheads took their dinner or supper to work with them. Those that didn't would slip over to the café.

Mr. Pilgrim, or R.O. as he was known, would push the vending wagon to the mill and serve the workers. R.O.'s wagon — known as the "dope-wagon," probably because of the "Goodies" powders, headache medicines, that were sold from it — was a plated steel contraption on wheels that kept the food warm and drinks cool. Pilgrim's was a typical southern café that served mainly hot dogs, hamburgers, and a few short-order meals. Memories still linger from the food served at Pilgrim's — it was that good. The cooks and servers behind the counter created a welcoming and comfortable atmosphere. It was always a treat and delight to visit Pilgrim's for a slaw dog, hamburger, the coldest soft drinks or, in the morning, fresh fried doughnuts.

As I ran to my house from Little Dink's, trying to outrun the sun and heat, I didn't even notice the sweat as it dripped from my body. I glanced at the cobble-like stone street, and my eyes became fixed on a shiny, new, Jefferson nickel. As I picked the nickel up, I quickly looked at our front door to see if Mama was there. She wasn't. I knew I was pretty much in the clear to visit the café at the bottom of the hill, probably 150 yards away.

I don't remember if the traffic light was red or not. I didn't care — I was thirsty and I had a nickel. I burst through the front door of the café and slid right up to the counter where Miss Elsie welcomed me with a smile.

Even though she was married, we still called her Miss Elsie. She lived on Highland Street. She knew all of us kids. She never met a stranger and always had a pleasant expression on her face.

"Well, well, well, who do we have here? Why are you in such a rush, son?" she asked.

"I need an RC, Miss Elsie." I puffed back.

"Wouldn't you rather have a Coca-Cola?" Miss Elsie asked.

"No, ma'am, they're too small. RC's have more, and I'm really thirsty." I said.

Miss Elsie started to giggle. I wasn't sure why, and right then I could care less. I just wanted a Royal Crown Cola. As Miss Elsie retrieved one from the drink chest, I quickly glanced at the top of Spring Street to see if Mama was there. I didn't see her so I felt safe, even though I knew deep down I was in the wrong. The drink chest kept the Cokes cold and icy. Mr. Pilgrim would place the bottles in the ice straight up so you could read the top of the drinks when you made your choice.

I placed the nickel on the counter as Miss Elsie rang the cash register. It quickly read ".05." She handed me the bottle, ten ounces instead of the six and a half ounce coke, and I raced to the opener to pry the lid off.

"Will, before you leave I want to tell you something," Miss Elsie offered. "When you look under the cap of the bottle, remove the cork, and if there is a red diamond on the cap you win a free RC."

I wasn't concerned at the moment about the red diamond. My luck expired when I found the nickel. Halfway up Spring Street and about midway through the bottle I remembered what Miss Elsie said. Most of us MilliKids carried a small pocket knife. I pried open the blade and commenced to scrape the cork cap protector off.

There it was — a red diamond. I couldn't believe it! Maybe it was a hallucination. It *was* terribly hot. Before I drank the RC, I had to be dehydrated (whatever that meant), but there was the diamond, there was Pilgrim's, and there was a near-empty RC bottle in my hand. I ran full speed, as fast as I could for another, yes another, free RC.

With another burst through the café door, Miss Elsie, in rare form, bent over in laughter.

"I knew you had a red diamond when I saw you with the cap and then your reaction. 'Will is on his way back'," she said.

"You know what I want, Miss Elsie. I am still thirsty."

"Here you are, son, now remember you can scrape that cork off, too, and if there is a red diamond, another free RC." She said.

"Yes, ma'am."

I didn't put any thought into it because I knew it wasn't going to happen again. As I left the café to carefully consider and prepare the story I had to concoct for Mama, I began to choke down another RC. Curious, I did pull out my knife once again and, before I even began to remove the cork, I thought that if perhaps there was another red diamond, I would race back over to Little Dink's to share my good fortune with him. He had shared with me on many occasions, and I figured this would be the least I could do for him.

As I savored the final drops of the coldest drink on the greatest day of my life, I removed the cork and then I knew I was in a dream. I couldn't believe it, another red diamond. I stood there on the sidewalk next to the gym, my eyes raced for our front porch, in the direction of Little Dink's house, and then I glanced back at the cafe.

My decision was easy, it was unselfish, it was admirable — and then I changed my mind and took off for the café one more time. Miss Elsie enjoyed every minute of it. I didn't realize it then, but I think she knew I was about to learn several important lessons. She had the RC ready, she took the red diamond, the empty bottle and she pointed in the direction of my house and said, "You better get home, son, I'm sure your mama is wondering where you are."

"Yes, ma'am."

I was full. I was no longer thirsty, mainly because there was no room. On my way up the hill I could see Stump's house, I could see Wart's house. Even though I couldn't see Little Dink's, I looked in his direction and remembered the promise I didn't keep.

I slowly crept up the front steps to our house when Mama came out the screen door.

"Where you been, boy?" she quipped in a sharp, bitter, tone.

"Well Mama, *ooh, ohh, ahrgh, ahrgh*," I began to vomit uncontrollably.

I continued to retch, and she stood there amused. She walked over to her porch swing and seemed to enjoy every minute. She was entertained, and it didn't cost her one nickel. She got all this for free.

After the hours it seemed to take for me to empty myself, she simply said, "I think you have learned your lesson."

She gave me a wet rag to cool my forehead and helped me to the lounge inside the living room. Not another word was spoken of that incident.

I have always believed that Miss Elsie called her, but I think mamas just know their children. What lesson did I learn? Besides the obvious, share your blessings with others.

Chapter 5
Pasture Surfing

It was fall, not a lot to do, but we always came up with something to occupy our time. I don't know why, but I just happened to look out our kitchen window and could see several of the MilliKids surfing down the long flowing grass that covered the hills below the standpipe. The standpipe, as we called it, was a huge, round tank that contained the natural spring water that supplied our homes. It was easily visible from most any point in New Holland and was situated on top of the hill in the pasture overlooking the village. Anyway, several of the kids had pieces of cardboard they had broken down to be used as a sled of sorts to slide down the grassy hill.

"Mama, can I go over to the pasture and play with those kids?" I asked as I pointed in the direction of the standpipe.

"Son, you don't have anything to slide on, and those kids are a little older than you. You better hang around here. I'm afraid you might get hurt," she said.

Feeling somewhat disappointed and left out, I just watched from a distance and envied the joyful shouts and youthful screams on the hillside. *What if I found a piece of cardboard, would she let me go then*? I asked myself. I knew the answer. The cardboard was her reason for me not going, but she actually didn't want me going by myself. She was overly protective that way, but I would eventually appreciate her insight in regards to my safety.

"Hey Will, you in there?" a familiar voice echoed through the living room.

"Yeah, be there in a second."

"Come on, Little Dink and me are going to the pasture," Stump blurted.

"Say it again a little louder so Mama can hear you," I said.

"Hey Wi…"

"I heard that, Stump. You just mind your own business and leave Will alone today," she said.

I was kind of hurt, but at the same time I always knew Mama had my best interests at heart. I stood at the kitchen door and watched Little Dink and Stump go join the fun. Usually, I could talk Mama into anything, but today she was a little more determined and cautious. It then occurred to me that Daddy and my brother, Butter, were not around.

"Where's Daddy and Butter?" I asked.

"They have gone to Sears and Roebuck and will be back in a little while," she answered.

For some reason, Daddy had left the ladder leaning against the roof next to the kitchen porch. I didn't bother asking Mama about it, I just climbed up on the roof above the kitchen to get a better look at all those kids having fun. The hill was covered with my friends, and it appeared that everyone was having a good time—that is, everyone but me. It wasn't long before Daddy and my brother came pulling up into the side yard where they parked the car. I noticed a huge box in the back seat, but I didn't have a clue what it could be.

"What are you doing on the roof...oh never mind just come help Daddy and me with this box," my brother said.

I climbed down and rushed to the car to see what was in the box. It had Zenith on the side and I knew right away we had bought a new TV. Too early for remote control and color, this was just another black-and-white television, but at least it was new and maybe had better reception. There were three channels available to us at the time, but we could only pick up two. Little did I know, but the quality of the TV had nothing to do with signal reception.

The TV was easy to set up, and in no time we were watching Dizzy Dean announcing the Yankees game—and people wonder why I am a Yankees fan even today. They were about the only regular team on TV during those years, and Mickey Mantle was in his prime. This day was getting better, little by little.

"Come on, Will," my brother urged. "Let's get on top of the house and adjust the antenna while Daddy fiddles with the TV."

That's the reason the ladder was already in place. Everyone knew we were getting a new TV but me, now we had to adjust the antenna to get better reception. My brother and I quickly scaled the ladder and repositioned the antenna.

"How is it, Daddy?" my brother asked. "Can you hear me? Is the reception better?"

Finally, Daddy came on the back porch and said, "The reception is much better, now come on down."

I was a little fearful about scaling down the ladder and my brother was becoming impatient with me.

"Hurry up, come on, hurry it up, I want to watch TV," he said.

The next thing I knew I was airborne off the roof with a little help from my brother. I didn't have time to be scared. I just braced for the collision with the earth below. A lot of questions were going through my mind. *Why would he do this? Did he really hate me this much? What did I do to upset him so?*

I bent my legs slightly and hit the ground hard, but I rolled and hopped back up. My brother remained on the roof laughing…

"I knew you wouldn't get hurt. It's not that long of a jump," he said.

I wasn't hurt. I was the one who usually got away with being somewhat mischievous, but not today. It was all Butter. I sat there, kind of shaken, but not injured.

"Why don't you just jump off then?" I shot back.

"Nope, I've got bad knees, can't take that chance."

I sat quietly a while longer, amazed at what I had just gone through. I was starting to feel a bit of pride and confidence that I certainly wasn't accustomed to, but it did feel good. Sometimes, I just had to be pushed to learn anything, and this was one of those days.

It dawned on me that my brother had actually pushed me down a hill so I wouldn't have any other option but to begin pedaling when I first learned to ride a bike. It was also my brother throwing me off the diving board at New Holland pool into the deep end that taught me swimming in the deep end is quite similar to swimming in the shallow. I had to be pushed sometimes. Honestly, I can't remember a time when it wasn't worth it. I didn't care for it at the time, but, looking back, I am grateful for my brother in seeing more ability in me than I saw in myself.

"Come here, son," Mama said. "You still want to go to the pasture and slide down those hills?"

"Yes, ma'am, you're not kidding are you?"

Mama laughed and said, "Here you go, now you have some cardboard, go have fun."

I had forgotten about the TV box. I quickly crushed it down, flipped open one end, turned one side up to hold on to, and off I went. I could still hear the hoots and shouts of my friends, and I couldn't wait to join the fun.

One of my childhood heroes, a non-athlete, but a hero nonetheless because of how he treated me and my family, was Tony. I called him Baloney. It seemed every time he came to visit my brother, they were closer in age, he had to eat whatever my brother was eating. Butter ate either a peanut butter or baloney sandwich, so Tony became Baloney.

"Hey Will," Baloney yelled. "Come up here and race me."

What a day this had turned out to be. There were at least ten kids now, and we had a ball. I can't really describe the sensation of flying down that hill on a piece of cardboard, but it was fast, smooth, and over with oh, so soon. We would get up and trudge back to the top of the hill to race again, being careful of others blazing the bent grass on their pieces of rugged board. We returned to the top over and over again that day. It was times like these that made the best memories. No one got hurt, and even those that did not have a board to soar on were invited to ride with someone or on a board that belonged to a friend.

We shared, we cared, we laughed, and we played until the sun went down and then some. Each day usually brought something different, but this was a special day indeed, pasture surfing and a new TV.

Chapter 6

Goodbye Is Never Easy

It was a sad day when Stan moved. Although his new home was about six miles up the road from New Holland, to me he was gone forever. Gone, in a sense I had never experienced before. I had yet to lose anyone in my family to death or relocation, but I did this day, and it would hurt for a long time.

Stan was my friend and one of only three boys our age in the same grade at school who lived on the same street. He was kind of tall, like me, but he carried himself with dignity and confidence that was not found in most of the school-aged children we were accustomed to being around. He was an athletic, good-looking boy who went to church every Sunday. I was jealous of him somewhat, but I was glad to call him *friend*.

"Hey, guess what, we're moving today," he said with a certain amount of excitement and pride.

"Where?" I asked, with an attempt to hide my shock.

"Just up the highway a few miles. We have built a new house on a piece of land Daddy bought, and we're to move today," he said.

My heart sank a little. I disguised my disappointment and sadness, just sort of covered it with an indifferent attitude so no one could see my pain. I actually hurt, it was like someone had removed a part of me and I wasn't prepared for what I heard. I am sure Stan didn't feel the same for me, but that's okay. We had spent several years together on the streets of New Holland and in the elementary school we attended. I looked up to Stan. He was always so confident and stood up to all the bullies in the village. He even took up for me on a couple of occasions.

"Where will you go to school?" I asked.

"I don't know yet. We still have a couple of weeks before school starts back, so I guess I'll find out then," he said.

"Well, so long," he said as he turned and headed back to his nearly empty house.

So this was it, this is how a relationship ends? What did we know? We were just kids, we didn't even know the right questions to ask or what to say to someone who was about to leave, someone you may never see again. All of a sudden, this day became quite miserable. Not even a handshake or words of farewell, just, "So long, see you one day."

I got up and slowly walked into my house and headed to my bedroom, where I would think and ponder for hours about what just occurred. I sat on my bed in the upstairs room wondering what will happen without Stan. *The world will never be the same.* I walked over to the front window and peered down onto Spring Street just as his car went by. He sat on the side where he could have easily looked up and seen me as I stared out the window, but he didn't. Obviously, he had other things on his mind, and our friendship wasn't one of them. I watched his car all the way to the bottom of Spring Street, as it turned left onto Cornelia Highway, and headed for his new home.

His car disappeared, and I didn't see Stan again for several years. We eventually played basketball against each other in elementary school, and in high school we were on the same team, but our relationship was never the same. When he left the village that day, he left, and both our lives would change forever.

"Are you okay, son? Didn't you know about their move?" My mom asked.

"No, no one told me. I hope we never have to move, Mama," I said. "It would be a terrible thing to leave all your friends behind and start over. That's something I never want to do."

I don't think Mama ever knew how hurt I was that day. Stan was my best friend, but I guess I wasn't his. I went to the window to look out again.

"Hey, Will, are you coming out today?" bellowed Little Dink, as he sat outside on his bike.

"Yeah, I'll be out in a minute," I responded.

Little Dink was a good friend, too. I guess he was my best friend now, but I found out soon enough I wasn't even his best friend either. MilliKids were close as kids, but as we grew older things changed, especially for the MilliKids. Little Dink, Wart, and Stump were all younger than I was. We really didn't allow the age difference to interfere with our fun, but it did make a difference from time to time. They sort of looked up to me more now that Stan was gone. He was the go-to guy, but I guess I replaced him, in a way. The problem for me was, who was going to be my go-to guy now, or did I need one?

I told the other kids about Stan's departure and it didn't seem to bother them. I found out why.

He didn't spend very much time with younger kids, and they felt like he ignored them and didn't consider them to be on his level. I didn't know it then, but our lives and took a sudden turn for the better. We trusted each other more and spent much, much more time together. A new pecking order had begun and with it came loads of fun. We became tighter as a group, and we grew closer as friends.

"Who do you think will move into Stan's old house?" Stump asked.

"It's about time for some good-looking girl to come along. God only knows we need help in this neighborhood," Little Dink added.

"Why are you so worried Little Dink? She won't have anything to do with you either. Your best chance is with one of the Chester sisters. Even you make one of them look good," remarked Stump.

"All I have heard is that a family from Branch Street will move in soon," Stump said. "And you know who lives on Branch Street? Nobody we want living over here."

"We'll see, we'll see, things have got to change for the better," Little Dink said.

A couple of days went by, and sure enough, two pickup trucks arrived loaded with furniture.

There were five people that included the mother and father (we assumed) that moved in. One of the boys looked about our age, but he pretended not to notice us. As usual, Stump volunteered to find out who they were.

"I'll find out who they are. Wait right here," he said, and continued to walk across the street.

Stump talked to the boy, who was our age, for a few minutes. He returned with his head hung low.

"They are the Cain family from Cleveland. There are two boys, ages ten and eight, and one girl, age six, with their mother. His name is Lace, and he is in the fourth grade. He said that his mom and dad would probably divorce, and they had to move away," Stump said. "Two nights ago, their house burned to the ground, and his mother blamed the father."

Everything the Cain family owned was destroyed. It wasn't long before neighbors in New Holland made sure they had food and extra clothing. Both the New Holland Methodist and Baptist churches chipped in and tried to make the Cain family welcome.

Lace was in my class that fall, and we became friends. He wasn't athletic, but he was interesting and intelligent. We included him in our day-to-day activities right from the start. A couple of weeks went by before I noticed that he hadn't been in school for a couple of days.

One afternoon, we were at Miss Icie's house when Little Dink came by and informed us that the Cain house was empty again. They had moved. We didn't know it. Lace didn't even say goodbye.

A few months passed. I picked up the daily newspaper and inside the front page was an article with Lace's picture on it. My heart raced as I began to read it. He and his mother, brother, and sister had moved back to Cleveland and reunited with their father. It was deer hunting season, and Lace helped to clean his father's gun. Lace didn't know it, but the gun was loaded and it discharged, killing him instantly. The loss of someone hurts, but somehow you must find a way to go on. Life is a mystery, but you surround yourself with people who care and mean a lot to you.

Chapter 7
Little Dink's Fall

    A warm spring evening had arrived and many of the older MilliKids decided to play fox-and-hounds. It's a game in which you choose sides and one team (the Hounds) count to a certain number, while the other team (the Foxes) finds a place to hide within a predetermined area. Once a hound finds a fox and grabs hold of him he must say, "Five, Ten, One-of-My-Men," and after doing so successfully, he then takes the fox back to base and guards him until the remainder of the team is caught. When the rest of the team is finally captured, they switch roles and start all over. It became one of our favorite games to play at night in the summer.

    The older kids were faster and sometimes a little meaner, which took away some of the fun. It made me reluctant to play because I usually wound up getting picked on since I was younger and much smaller. However, if you didn't participate they would often tease you anyway. This night was one of the first times Little Dink had joined us. He was several years younger than most, including me, but he was always fun to be around. Teams had been chosen, and Little Dink and I were on the same team. We were the Foxes during round one, so we were the first to hide.

"Hey Will, stay with me, will you?" Little Dink pleaded.

I didn't know if he was scared or just wanted to be near someone with whom he was more familiar. Anyway, we kept close and ran to a great spot. Little Dink giggled when he was nervous or unsure about himself, and tonight he was more nervous than usual. We found our way to the hedges between our house and the Ferleys. They were a family that lived behind us and adjacent to Highland Avenue. Ordinarily, Mr. Ferley did not like us to play in his yard. He would often tell us to go somewhere else, but his hedges were so private and provided protection when needed.

"Little Dink, you've got to stay quiet or they'll find us," I said as I choked down a giggle. "You'll give us away, and we won't stay free long. Besides, we know the best places to hide and as small as we are we'll be trouble to find. Now hush."

"Will, do you—*hehe, glump glump glump…*"

"Shh, settle down, we are safe but – *hehehe*. Oh my goodness, don't get me going," I pleaded.

A couple of hounds walked by, so I covered Little Dink's mouth and pulled him tight to muffle his giggles. He settled down a little, but both of us were ready to burst out with a laugh.

"Here," I said as I reached into my pocket for a piece of Bazooka bubble gum. "Maybe this will keep you still and quiet."

I had one piece of gum from earlier in the day, and I broke it in half to share with him. Bazooka was made to be shared, it was that good. It had a crease down the middle of it to help make it easier to split into two pieces.

"Let me read the cartoon," Little Dink begged.

Each piece of gum had a short cartoon about Bazooka Joe and a fortune, which was usually corny, but it was something that made us read and wonder. Anyway, Little Dink was insistent as he read the cartoon.

"Hey guys, slide over." It was Stump. One of the captains put him on our team. They had given Stump a few extra minutes to hide.

"How did you know we were here?" I asked.

"You can hear Little Dink's giggles and snorts a block over. After all, I know where your secret places are. It's a good thing, maybe, that I'm on your team. You got any more of that gum, Will?"

"That's all we need, for you guys to laugh and blow bubbles, better yet, to pop bubbles, when we need to hide. You'll give us away if you don't stay still and silent," I pleaded again.

"Come on, gimme some gum," Stump kept on.

"If you'll keep a lid on it and settle down, I'll sneak into my house and get another piece," I said.

"Hurry up, they'll be here before long," Stump said.

Somehow a beam from the street lamp seeped through the hedges into our secret place.

"Give me Bazooka Joe's cartoon, Will. I can read it thanks to the street light," Little Dink begged.

I had just stepped on the side porch of our house when I heard both of them start to laugh after they read the cartoon. I went to the cabinet where I hid things from my brother and his friends. Candy and other goodies just weren't safe in my house, but I had Bazooka Joe hidden fairly well. I eased back to the side porch. As I headed back to our spot, I heard Little Dink and Stump start to laugh as they ran. The Hounds had found them and gave chase through our backyard.

Suddenly, I got the giggles as I watched these two idiots outrun much bigger kids. They were successful for about thirty seconds when…

"Five, ten, one-of-my-men" erupted from the mouths of the two hounds who had caught Little Dink and Stump. Even after their capture, they still giggled, snorted, and laughed all the way to base, which was located under the street lamp at the intersection of Highland and Spring streets. One of the rules of fox-and-hounds is that an un-captured team member can run to base, and tag a teammate's hand to free him until he is caught again. That was my plan, so I laid low for a while. The Hounds had put another one of my friends in charge of the prisoners at the base. If he were to detect someone close by (like I was about to be) to free the prisoners, he could yell for help. I was about to sprint toward the base and free my friends, when, out of nowhere, came Lurch. He was an older MilliKid and one of our teammates. Lurch was clumsy and quite awkward, but here he came to save the day for Little Dink and Stump. At about the same moment, he touched their hands to free them, the base guard screamed for help. Lurch stumbled as he freed Little Dink, Stump was recaptured because Lurch fell on him when he tried to escape, and Lurch was captured as well.

It's almost impossible to run and laugh out loud at the same time, but I was doing my best. I decided to follow Little Dink. He had Big Ben, another MilliKid, close on his tail, and I mean close, so I ducked behind a tree in front of Mr. Ferley's house.

"You can't catch me, Big Ben, not tonight, I'm too fast," Little Dink taunted as he rounded Mr. Ferley's house.

"When I do catch you I'm going to teach you a lesson, you little rat," Big Ben snapped back.

I couldn't believe what happened next. Fifty years later, it still gives me goose bumps. As Little Dink ran, he suddenly tripped and fell head first onto the walkway in front of Mr. Ferley's house. His head hit the curb and he lay motionless. We all screamed. Blood was everywhere. Big Ben picked Little Dink up and took him home. Blood had saturated Big Ben's shirt. Our game had ended — a MilliKid was hurt. Little Dink never lost consciousness. As a matter of fact, he even spoke some while Big Ben rushed him home. Above his eye was a huge split that required stitches. Almost every MilliKid had stitches at one time or another. To brag, you better have more than three or four stitches and a gruesome story to go with it.

As everyone discovered what happened, they rushed to Little Dink's house to check on him. His mom and dad were calm. They gathered the car keys and took him to the hospital immediately. Little Dink had a big smile on his face and enjoyed the attention. He had blood all over him, all over Big Ben, and all over Mr. Ferley's sidewalk.

The next day, there was a knock at my door. It was Little Dink and Stump.

"You ever had seven stitches, Will," Little Dink snickered. "What a night, huh?"

"Are you okay? It scared me to death, blood was everywhere," I said.

"Yeah, I'll be fine," he said as he handed me a small piece of paper.

It was the Bazooka Joe gum wrapper. The cartoon wasn't that funny, but the fortune, we will never forget… *Be a Friend to Someone who needs a Friend.*

Chapter 8
Gillespie's Bus

Saturday mornings in the village were always special. Whether it was during the school year or in the months of summer, the MilliKids couldn't wait for Saturday to arrive. We usually had our weekends planned the day before, but we were always ready for the unexpected and spontaneous goings-on of the weekend.

Every Saturday morning a local grocery store, a mom and pop brand, Gillespie's, would send their converted school bus to our village to deliver groceries. Now, mind you, it wasn't just a rolling supermarket, it was a monstrous vehicle that usually took up the whole street, but, boy, was it a welcomed sight, especially if any of us had a little change in our pockets. Gillespie's knew that the mill villages in the area were populated with people who had spent a minimum of forty hours during the preceding week working in the mill. Everyone was tired, some were already too old to travel far. But more importantly, everyone needed groceries or other supplies, and they usually found it on the bus. Like I said, it was a welcomed sight, and we waited patiently for its arrival.

There it came at its usual time, rolling down Highland Avenue. We knew its stops. We had to wait patiently because it was so deliberate in moving from stop to stop. It ambled across Spring Street, staying on Highland until it reached Myrtle Drive, and for whatever reason unbeknownst to us, it came to a laboring stop in front of the Brownlow residence, always in front of the Brownlows.

Now that I think about it, it probably stopped there because so many people lived in the Brownlow house—too many to count actually. Anyway, we ran to it, with great anticipation of the indescribable cinnamon and peppermint aroma that permeated the bus. People sauntered through their front doors making their way to the "rolling store." Here came the Brownlows, and it seemed like there were thirty of them shuffling through the front door one at a time. *Where could all these people sleep?* I thought to myself. My goodness, Gillespie's must have made a fortune just from this one stop alone. My friends and I knew that there was no reason for us to try and board the bus, no room. Too many Brownlows.

"Now you boys just be patient and wait for me to get my things," Ole Lady Stover would say to us predictably every Saturday. "I'll be finished in a few minutes, just wait right there."

Ole Lady Stover didn't like me, and she didn't care for any of my friends either. She was always mean and fussy. She lived across the street from the Brownlows.

Gillespie's Bus

I don't know why I was in such a hurry. I didn't have a cent on me, but it was an experience just to walk on the bus and pretend like you could buy anything you wanted. The smell, I can't describe it, spices, cinnamon, and oranges, all mixed together made my throat water.

Little Dink was already on the curb when the bus pulled up, he always had money. I believe his mom and dad made sure he had some change, just to get him out of the house.

"What have you got on your mind today, Will?" Little Dink asked.

"I don't know, maybe a Reese's or York Pattie." I said. I didn't have any money to spend. But it was fun to pretend. Reese's (We called them "Reecie's," peanut butter surrounded with chocolate), or a York Peppermint Pattie were my favorites. I would have to invent some lie when it came time to board the bus, but I could dream until then.

"Boy, I can't wait," Stump sputtered as he slid onto the bank where we were sitting, "I've got twenty-five cents, and I'm going to spend it all."

Just us three, that was okay, sometimes the other kids caught the bus on an earlier stop. They probably made sure they got their goodies before the bus reached the Brownlow house. You took a chance by waiting on the Brownlows. Sometimes there wasn't much left when they finished. Maybe I'd start meeting the bus earlier, if for no other reason than to avoid Ole Lady Stover.

There were probably three or four adults on the bus, and we were waiting for them to exit. They did finally, and now it was our time. For some reason, other than not having any change, I just sat still and waited for Little Dink and Stump to return. Surely I would have a good enough excuse by then to satisfy their curiosity as to why I remained outside.

I could hear Little Dink and Stump talking on the bus. I didn't know the driver. I just reckoned he must have been a Gillespie. Anyway, he just drove. Someone else was usually in charge of taking in the money as people made their purchases. The act of providing a service is a virtue that is certainly missing in the world today, but Gillespie's did indeed serve the people of New Holland and other surrounding neighborhoods.

Here came Little Dink with a Coke and Butterfinger, and Stump had a drink and candy bar as well. You might think that all we did was eat junk food. Well, we did when we could, but it was seldom, once a week maybe, and only if you had the money to spend. None of us MilliKids had the luxury of junk food in our homes. I say luxury (and it was for us), but today junk food haunts us everywhere we turn. There is either a machine or store that has just about anything, for just about anybody, for just about any price.

"Aren't you going to buy something today, Will?" Little Dink asked.

"Naw, I think I'll just wait until next week. By then they'll have something I want." I answered.

Little Dink had this look on his face. I didn't want anyone to feel sorry for me, but I could tell he knew the truth because he knew me so well.

"I have an extra dime, Will. You can pay me back next week," he offered.

Little Dink was like that. More than once he offered to treat me. I really wanted to take his dime, but I couldn't. I thanked him any way.

He and Stump sat and enjoyed their snacks while I remembered thinking, *Will my life ever be different? Why is it, some people always seemed to have money, but I seldom do.* Anyway, after I had my own pity party, both of them tried again to share their goodies with me, and again I refused.

"Thanks, guys, but I can't," I said. "It's time for lunch, and I believe I hear Mama calling. See you in a little while."

Mama didn't call. It was my excuse to leave before self-pity took over. I rose to my feet and began a long and lonesome walk home. Many, many, many times during my childhood I often wondered if my life would ever be different. What a difference a quarter would make. I knew Mama had on a pot of pinto beans, cornbread, slaw, pickled beets, and sweet iced tea for lunch. We didn't have much, but it was enough and she was a terrific cook. She might even have on a pot of blackberry cobbler. Still, I felt pitiful, but I didn't want sympathy.

"You better be good and hungry," she said.

I was and, boy, was it good, but no cobbler.

After lunch, I went on the front porch to swing and wait for my buddies to come over. For some reason, Little Dink and Stump walked around the far end of the church across the street. I didn't think much of it at the time. They had these goofy smiles on their faces, like they had just done something stupid, which was quite typical for them, and they hastened their steps to our front porch.

"Did you have a good lunch?" Little Dink asked.

"Yeah, did you get enough to eat?" Stump chimed in.

"Yes, I did, what are you two up to? Something's going on," I said.

"Here, Will, we know how it feels, and it doesn't feel good when someone else eats and enjoys something in front of you," Little Dink said as he extended his hands.

It was a brown paper bag containing a Reese's and Coke.

"We were able to scrape up a few more coins and chase the bus down on Victor Street to get you a snack," Stump said. "We felt bad eating in front of you, and we knew you didn't have any money. But you better pay us back some day," as both of them laughed.

It means more to me today, fifty years later, than it did then, but it taught me a lifelong lesson — to share. Whatever your good fortune may be, spread it around. One day when the memories are almost gone, you'll be able to recall times like these where the seemingly small things in the world made a huge difference.

Chapter 9
Big Dink's Peppers

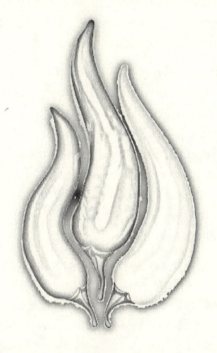

New Holland had its share of characters living in the duplexes the mill had built at the turn of the century, and none more flamboyant, eccentric, and, yes, scary, than Ole Man Seymour. Fondly known as "Big Dink," he lived on Highland Avenue, and was guided and urged by his own set of indulgences, but we won't get in to those just yet. I never really understood what Big Dink did for a job. Maybe he didn't. He always seemed to have a headache. When the MilliKids would come close to his proximity, he would often insist (in his special vernacular) for us to get the heck away from his house. We did, no questions asked. We understood he wasn't in any mood to put up with our shenanigans. However, when he was in a good mood, and we never really knew what put him in a good mood, he wasn't half-bad to be around.

This particular day was, again, quite hot and humid. There were five of us on this Saturday morning. Let me introduce you to Rusty. Rusty wasn't really a MilliKid, even though he would have done anything to be around us every day. His aunt, uncle, and grandmother lived in New Holland, and he would visit every week. Rusty's family roots were in the village, so whenever he came by he was always included. He was one of us, so I guess he earned the right to be called a MilliKid.

We chose up sides for a game of Monopoly, and it wound up with Little Dink and me as partners, against, Stump, Wart, and Rusty. This wasn't the first time Little Dink and I had played against them, we were masters of manipulation, especially who won. I won't say Little Dink and I cheated or even fudged, but we knew how to manipulate the rules and outcome to our advantage. We wouldn't make it too obvious, but we knew how to keep it close so there wouldn't be any questions.

"Come on, come on, come on," Stump urged to get the game going. "I have to get a haircut today, and I don't have much time."

As usual, the MilliKid who lived in the house where we played would be the banker, as if that mattered to Little

Dink and me. We had our signals and, even though we were highly suspect at times, no one was ever the wiser. Today, we were at Little Dink's house, and he loved to be the banker. The game was in the bag, so we thought. Little did we know, Little Dink's dad, Big Dink, was watching. As soon as Little Dink had dealt the money, Big Dink noticed a few extra 500 and 100 dollar bills in his son's stack. It would be too obvious for Little Dink to bolster my stash a little as well, but he was my partner, and I knew his intentions. When I did run short, Little Dink always found a way to slip me a couple of his bills. Big Dink didn't say anything at first, I was surprised he even noticed, but he was about to put an end to our little flim-flam and spoil our day.

"Would you roll the dice?" urged Wart.

With the back of his hand Little Dink playfully slapped Wart in the back of the head just to get his attention. The dice were rolled, and the game began. Before long, we had a true monopoly on Park Place and Boardwalk, the game was essentially over.

"Boys, do y'all like peppers?" Big Dink asked.

I was quick to raise my hand because I did like peppers, but Wart raised his hand, too, and the fun was about to begin.

"Come with me to my garden in the backyard, and I'll give you some," he said.

Stump decided it was time for his haircut so he went home. MilliKids didn't walk anywhere. We usually ran or biked — we flew to our next destination unless it was chore time. Wart and I quickly got up and followed Big Dink to his garden.

"Boys, be real careful now when you walk between the rows and not step on any of my goodies, okay?" he said.

"Okay."

We stayed close to Big Dink, and about the fifth or sixth row in we saw his peppers, and they were tempting. Bright red and bright green, not bell peppers but hot peppers. We just didn't know how hot. Big Dink had picked one to eat, and then he picked another off the vine for us. He smiled and chewed on his pepper which made me think he rather enjoyed it, so why not?

"Thanks, it really looks good and tasty." I said.

"Yeah, thanks," Wart said.

One thing we MilliKids learned early in life was when you got something out of the ground, off the vines, or out of fruit trees, before you could actually start to enjoy whatever treat it was, first you had to spit on it to clean it.

Wart and I took a big bite off a pepper about the same time. What happened next words cannot begin to describe or explain. Immediately, the sensation cascaded my lips, tongue, throat, stomach, nose, nostrils, neck, eyes, and even the hair on top of my head. I couldn't breathe, I couldn't see, I couldn't smell, but I could run — and I ran as fast as I could. My eyes were full of tears, not from pain but from the fiery, searing flames that coursed from my head to my

Big Dink's Peppers

toes. I was on fire. Somebody needed to call the fire department and call them fast.

The distance between Little Dink's house and mine was about 200 yards, and ordinarily it would take a minute or so to get home. But not this day. I wasn't worried about traffic on Highland Avenue or Spring Street, where I lived. I couldn't see anyway, but I knew the way home. I had to get to Mama.

"Yeoow, aargh, yeow," I could hear Wart in the background, but I wasn't worried about him at the moment—I was worried about me.

How could anything be this hot? I don't remember making any noise, although I am sure I did. All I had on my mind was Mama and ice water. I left Spring Street aimed at our screened-in kitchen door, it couldn't have been more than two or three leaps before I was at the kitchen sink. I drank water, which did not help; ice from the fridge, which did not help; a stick of butter, which did not help. I finally resorted to the spigot in the backyard and lay down under it for what seemed like hours. I let it run on my mouth, head, nose, ears, everywhere, it didn't matter. Relief was slow in coming. It finally wore off.

When I returned to the kitchen I could see Big Dink a block away. He laughed so hard he had to sit in the grass to catch his breath. Neighbors had gathered next to him as he told the story.

Mama tried her best not to laugh, and the more she tried not to, the madder I became. *Why would anyone do this to a kid?* But where was Wart? I went across our backyard to Wart's house, but he was not to be found. I remembered that his mom and dad were not at home, and he didn't have a key to get in. So, where was he?

Suddenly, on the next street over, Tower Street, I saw him as he ran down toward the main highway. I gave chase. He'd tried to run the heat off. He actually thought the pepper was going to kill him. I caught him and tried to somewhat give comfort, but he was in a panic. Nothing I could say or do would be of any help. Finally, I convinced him to come to my house for some ice water. By the time we got to my kitchen porch, he had settled down quite a bit. We sort of looked at each other, looked toward Ole Man Seymour's house, and started to laugh. We had never experienced anything like this before.

Mama saw us in the side yard and brought us each a popsicle — if for no other reason than to give us a little refreshment to ease our humiliation. MilliKids, for the most part, could laugh at themselves, because it really was funny once we got over the personal part and realized no harm was done or intended. We never thought any less of Big Dink. As a matter of fact, it gave us something to talk and laugh about for the next few days and weeks. After all, we were the MilliKids, and we were always doing something stupid — so it seemed.

Chapter 10
Never Enough

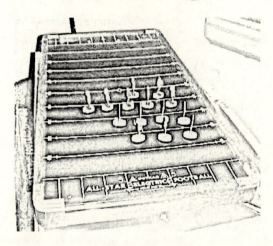

Christmas came once a year and that was a tough wait. Many children celebrate birthdays almost the same as they do Christmas, but not my family. The main difference was the number of gifts we received. We were lucky if we got more than one gift for our birthday. It might have happened on occasion, but usually just one gift and not a big one at that. So, Christmas was special for a child in a mill village. My parents made sure I had plenty of gifts on Christmas morning—not Christmas Eve, only on Christmas morning.

I guess, for most kids it was nearly impossible to fall asleep on Christmas Eve. It was for me every year, but eventually I would wake to an unforgettable day. Mama, always an early riser, had the smell of bacon sifting through the house. I can still smell it today. She was a wonderful cook.

"Okay boy, you've got to eat first before you go into the living room," she would always say.

Every Christmas morning we had to eat first. Santa had already left presents under the tree, but ordinarily there were many other presents Mama and Daddy had bought. It was a special day, even for them. They found a way to provide even when they couldn't really afford it. I never knew how they paid all the bills, but they did and that made Christmas even more exciting, unforgettable, and all the more special.

"Sit down over there, near the heater, and keep warm while I fix you a plate," she said.

It seemed like this was the same scenario every Christmas. Most of my friends celebrated on Christmas Eve. We had to wait until morning, but then the wait was always worth it—except for this morning—something was different.

My brother was not home any more(being seven years older he was married now) and I was the only child left. (My sister, who was twelve years older, had gotten married and left many years earlier.) I was alone, and Christmas changed forever. The joy was gone…almost.

What I didn't know, but soon realized, was that my family's finances were at the lowest point ever. My mom had been stricken with cancer and wasn't able to work any longer. She had medical and pharmaceutical bills, which drained the bank account. This Christmas was going to be a Christmas to remember because the Christmas tree was almost bare. I thought Santa had simply forgotten about us, *or me*. Yes, let's keep Santa in this picture. In many ways, he was the real culprit in all of this.

I do remember a couple of gifts. One of them was the latest magnetic football game that operated off electricity, and I believe the only other gift I got was a new baseball glove. Yes, I was disappointed. I had to act proud, excited, and overjoyed at these meager gifts. I pretended that the magnetic football game was one of the coolest presents I had ever received. It wasn't, and, pray tell, what was I going to do with a new baseball glove during the winter? I felt so sorry for myself. I believe I got a little mad, but I didn't let on, my mom and dad never knew how hurt I was that morning. My mom's pain and suffering from radiation and cobalt treatments from her bout with cancer didn't matter to me at that point. This quickly became the worst Christmas ever.

Christmas was always about me, I thought.

I didn't even like football that much, but I tried to enjoy the game, it just never operated quite right. Anyway, a knock on the door...

"Hey Will, what did you get?" a blustery voice yelled out.

It was Little Dink, and he had to show me his new bike. It was a beauty, green with specks of silver on it, long and sleek, with a horn and headlight. He was barely big enough to ride it.

"Come on in," I said, "I have a new football game we can play."

Little Dink came in and immediately forgot about his bike. He plugged in the game and placed the magnetic players on the metal field and began to play like he had done it before.

"This is great, what else did you get?" he asked.

I showed him my baseball glove, but he wasn't interested in it. He went back to the football game. Here he sat with a new bike outside, and he's more excited about this dumb football game. I wondered for a moment if he might like to trade me the bike for this game…no such luck. I didn't have the heart to ask for fear of hurting Mama's feelings.

About that time, Little Dink and I heard a distinct sound of a small motor coming from the street in front of my house. We raced to the door and "*vroom, vroom*" went one of the older kids in the neighborhood down the street on a go-cart. Envy welled up in me so fast I thought I was going to explode.

"That's James, he's been up and down every street in New Holland and probably in most of the backyards as well," Little Dink said. "I'm already sick of him showing off on his new cart."

"Hey, look, there's Stump across the street next to the church; he's got a BB gun," Little Dink said. "That's one thing I will never have to bother asking my parents for, a BB gun. They have made it clear that a gun is not in my future."

"See if you can hit one of Little Dink's tires on his bike, Stump. Take a shot, he won't mind," I said as we all chuckled.

Never Enough

"I've got something in the house you can take target practice on," I sort of joked about the football game. "You can put it and me out of my misery."

We had crossed the street to the church steps to watch Stump shoot and Little Dink pedal. At least the day had gotten a little better.

"Here he comes again, take aim and see if you can hit James on his go-cart; that might slow him down or at least make him stay on his end of the street," Little Dink said.

"Let me have the gun before you get us all in trouble," I said.

I grabbed it away in a playful manner and noticed something peculiar—it had no BB's in it. Stump gave me this befuddled look and then it occurred to me...the gun was empty.

"Have you already shot up all of your BB's?" I asked.

He remained silent with no expression.

"What good is a BB gun if you don't have any BB's?" Stump asked angrily.

"Do you mean you don't have any BB's?" Little Dink asked with a giggle.

"I am so mad at my parents. They said until I get all my chores done, my room cleaned, and the house swept, I won't get any BB's. I had to get out of there."

Little Dink and I started to laugh. We couldn't catch our breaths. Stump was getting madder by the minute at us, but we didn't care. Christmas was getting better and better.

We turned around to go back to my house and here came Wart with something strange next to his ear. We couldn't make it out at first. We thought maybe it was a transistor radio, but when he came closer we discovered he had a Walkie Talkie.

"Mama, will you turn the thing on!" Wart screamed into the side of the Walkie Talkie. "Good gosh, woman, turn it on, I said!"

"How do you expect her to hear you if she doesn't have hers turned on, Wart?" I gently asked.

I had no sooner gotten these words out of my mouth when we began to laugh again. Here he was, a full block away from his house, and his screams echoed through the village because he thought his mother could hear him. Wart never took to laughter very well, so he turned and ran home with the Walkie Talkie still close to his ear. By the end of the day, all four of us had gathered in my front room to play football. We had a great time after all.

MilliKids were spoiled, but when it came to simply having fun and being thankful and grateful, we were blessed in more ways than one. I learned that it doesn't take a lot of money to make Christmas special. It simply takes people and parents who care. I know that my parents did the most they could with what little they had. The football game served its purpose that day. It taught me to understand that Christmas is about Jesus and those you care about and love.

Chapter 11

Mr. Pete and Mr. Manley

Everyone I knew could swim, better yet, dive. Not me. I was basically afraid of the water. It was spring, and the pool was soon to open for the season. All the kids in the village were excited and couldn't wait to get wet. Why not? We were blessed with an indoor community pool, located in the gym underneath the basketball court. My main fear (and I had several) was water. I did not want to put my head under. Feet first, only up to my chest, that was my limit…enter Mr. Pete.

Mr. Pete was our local, homegrown coach and athletic mentor. He could do anything related to sports. I never had a chance to thank him for all he did, not only for practically every boy and girl in the community, but also for me. Mr. Pete's main job was in the mill. I remember him as he walked to and from work every day. His occupation...not sure. His purpose...to enrich kids' lives in New Holland without any expectations. He taught us all how to swim. That's where I enter.

"Come on, chicken! At least you can jump in; it's not going to kill you," Greg chided.

Greg was a classmate, and sometimes a bully. There were several in this class who made my life miserable for years. He, Johnny, and Double G found it amusing to poke fun at me, and did so relentlessly. They didn't realize it, (nor did I) but they helped build my character, which will serve me eternally. I wish I had known and understood it then — perhaps life wouldn't have been as daunting.

"It's okay, Will. There was a time when they didn't know how to swim either. They're just making fun of you because you remind them of themselves not too long ago," Mr. Pete reassured.

Mr. Pete knew me and my family very well. He was not a big man. But he had a huge heart, one that I will never forget.

"Go ahead and jump in. I'll be here to grab you, just in case," Mr. Pete said kindly.

Just in case of what? I thought and spoke quietly to myself.

So I jumped. Three feet deep, that's all, and it was so warm and inviting. It felt terrific. The pool was heated by

Mr. Pete and Mr. Manley

steam created by a boiler in the back room next to the dressing area.

"You three, grab the overflow wall on this end, you three, the same thing on that side of the pool, and you three, on the other side of the pool," he ordered nicely.

Mr. Pete's tone of voice was always soothing, reassuring, and safe. Almost as if he knew what we needed most—a dose of special attention. Even though this was a physical education class for students at New Holland Elementary, Mr. Pete taught swimming and a host of other sports for the school.

"Now each of you stretch out, pick your feet and legs up to the surface, and begin to kick, but make sure you continue to hold onto the water trough for safety," he instructed.

I looked around to make sure I was doing it right, and there was my friend Terry on the other side still in shock. To see him in that position made me feel better about myself.

Mr. Pete moved gently from one student to the next with words of encouragement and simple instruction as he taught. It was difficult for me to keep my legs and feet high enough to kick, but Mr. Pete held my legs up allowing me to see that I could stay above water just by making these rapid movements. Within moments we all caught on and realized we had learned to float.

"Hey look, Will can float now! Come join us at the diving board," Greg heckled.

"Yeah, come on down, Will, and join the big boys, ha-ha," Johnny thundered.

At the other end of the pool were the older students who could swim and dive without help. There were even girls down there, which added to my embarrassment. Shame came easy for me, but again, character is built from negative experiences that turn into positive memories, and this was one of them. I just didn't know it at the time.

"This is fun, ain't it, Will?" Terry barked as he turned to face me.

Mr. Pete had us turn and with our hands and arms behind our heads so we could look across the pool. We still held on to the overflow trough and swiftly kicked our legs and feet, belly-side up. "Now, everyone stand up straight in the pool and watch as Will goes from one side of the pool to the other," Mr. Pete said. "Will, reach out in front of you as if you are grabbing the trough and lift your legs and feet and begin to kick,"

All of a sudden, I was at the other side of the pool and I felt like the King of the World. This was one of the greatest moments of my life. Everyone watched, and I had done the impossible.

Shortly, all of the students were going from side to side and then, without further instruction, we flailed our arms and suddenly realized we had learned to swim.

"Hey Will, way to go, you've got it now," Ron said as he clapped for me.

Mr. Pete and Mr. Manley

Ron was my friend. The bullies didn't mess with him. He was a hero to me then, but became an even greater hero in just a few short years, not only to me, but to this country. He was the only boy in that pool that wound up dying for us all. He was killed in Vietnam in June 1967.

"That's not bad, that's not bad," encouraged Greg. He later would serve this country in Vietnam also, but he survived. He never bullied me again.

After school, I ran home, up the front steps, and burst through the front door yelling, "I can swim, I can swim, I can swim!"

"Oh yeah, but can you dive?" My brother Butter had to spoil the day.

He had this unusual sense and knew how to annoy me when it hurt the most, but this time I didn't let him bother me.

"That's later. Right now, I feel like a fish! I can't wait to go to the pool this evening," I bellowed.

Daddy didn't say much, and Mama just smiled. The smile was enough. I was accustomed to Daddy's quietness, but I knew he was pleased—I guess.

The day passed by slowly, and I had already told Little Dink and Stump what had happened but they were not amused.

"I thought you could already swim," Little Dink said.

"Are you guys going to the pool when it opens this evening?" I asked.

"No, not me. I've got other things to do. Besides Mama won't let me go without Daddy, and he's at work," Stump said.

"Probably not me either," Little Dink added.

It was 5:00 p.m. and the pool was open. I could see kids as they arrived on bikes and got out of cars with their parents. I rushed into the house and found Mama.

"Will you go with me, Mama?" I pleaded.

"Why, of course, son, just give me a moment," she said.

We walked to the gym and through the front door. I rushed to the dressing room while she found a seat where spectators could watch. I quickly undressed, rinsed off and emerged onto the pool decking. Mother had already paid the lifeguard, Mr. Manley, fifteen cents for my admission. I slowly walked to the far end of the pool, where it was only three feet deep, and crept down the steps ever so gently. Again, the water was warm and invigorated me. It felt wonderful.

"Watch, Mama," I hollered from the shallow end.

I remembered what Mr. Pete had taught me and swam from side to side. I could tell she was pleased as she continued to talk with Mr. Manley. They had known each other for many years. I stepped out of the pool to get her attention and jumped in the deep end of the pool so she would notice. I remember going under, but not touching the bottom. I started to panic when Mr. Manley jumped in and pulled me out.

"Good try, Will," Mr. Manley said as he tried to reduce my fright, "but you better stay at the other end until you get used to this deep end, okay?"

"Yes, sir," as I wiped tears from my eyes.

Most people probably thought it was just water, but they were tears.

"My boy can swim; way to go son," Mama encouraged.

I hurried back to the shallow end. I didn't realize until many years later that Mr. Manley saved my life. I never thanked him. I don't know if Mama or Daddy did either. I assume they did. Anyway, one of the greatest days in my life almost turned into my last.

Chapter 12
Shattered Dream

"Hey Will, you get to ride on James' go-cart yet?" Little Dink asked. "I have. Boy, was it fun. That James sure is a nice guy."

"Where did you go on it?" I asked.

"Oh, he took me–" he started.

"You mean you didn't get to drive it yourself?" I interrupted.

"No…he said I was too young, but he would take me down Highland, across the garden to Spring, and then back up to my house," Little Dink continued. "Go ask him. Maybe he'll give you a ride."

"I don't want to ride with him, I want to drive it myself," I said. "Anyway, I don't think James really likes me, so I don't need to ride in it anyway."

It's not that I was envious or jealous, but in a way I was. Life just didn't seem fair at times. James was one of the older MilliKids (certainly not one of us), but was spoiled rotten just like Wart. As a matter of fact, they were a lot alike, which made it easier to understand why kids like them often got just about anything they wanted.

"Little Dink, do you ever think you'll have your own go-cart?" I asked.

"Probably not. Daddy thinks I'll either kill myself or someone else if I had one," he said.

"He's right about that; you are too crazy to have a go-cart. I can see you now as you rush through every stop sign and ignore all the laws — except the ones you create," I said. "Either way, I don't believe you or me will ever have a go-cart of our own."

I was near Little Dink's house when all of this was going on. I turned around to go home and noticed Stump sitting on our front porch as he waited for me. I picked up my pace and hurried there.

"What's going on, Stump, where you been all day?" I asked.

"Just bored, nothing much to do, and I am so sick of James racing up and down our street acting like he owns it. You know, I could sneak over to his house and let the air out of his tires once he takes a break. I don't think he's ever going to give that thing a rest. Surely, he gets hungry," Stump grumbled.

"Wait a second," I said quietly. "He's got to run out of gas sooner or later. Wouldn't it be cool if he ran out at the bottom of one of these hills? You know he's not going to push that thing home."

Mama came through the screened-in front door. At the same time, Wart dashed around the side of our house (Wart didn't walk anywhere—he always ran, usually from someone or something). Mama sat in her usual spot, on the swing, and Wart plopped down beside Stump and joined our little plan to upset James' day.

"What are you, I mean *we*, up to now?" Wart asked. "I can tell something's on your mind, and you two are up to no good."

We retraced our conversation. The only difference was that Mama heard every word and didn't like any of it.

"Boys, I'll tell you right now, you're headed for trouble," she announced. "Stay away from James and stay away from his go-cart. They're too dangerous."

Mama got up to go in the house, and when I glanced up at her she had this peculiar look on her face. I wasn't sure I had ever seen that look before, but it had my attention. Anyway, I quickly refocused our thoughts on today's agenda.

"Sounds like it's time for a baseball game," I said. "Are you guys up to it?"

We could still hear James as he roared up and down Highland and around Spring to Myrtle Drive and back. We all wished one of us was on that go-cart.

"I tell you what, Stump, you go to Little Dink's house and get him and anybody else you see. And Wart, you run over to Carolina and see if Rusty is there and we'll meet back here in thirty minutes. I'm going to eat lunch and get most of the equipment together for our game."

A ball and bat. Not many of us had gloves so we usually played with a hard rubber ball so no one would get hurt. As I walked into the house, Mama hung up the phone. She had talked with one of her friends.

"Son, come here a moment. Let me tell you what I want to do. I know you would do anything for a go-cart…"

"Yes, ma'am, anything, anything in this world! What are you saying, what are you saying, what are you saying?" I bellowed.

"Hold on a sec…I just got off the phone with Miss Etty, and she thinks she knows where I can get you a go-cart we can afford," she went on.

Miss Etty was one of Mama's friends.

"Don't get your hopes up. It probably won't work out, but Miss Etty and I are going to go look at the cart this afternoon…like I said…don't get your hopes up," Mama said softly.

She had no more uttered these words when, I suddenly burst through the screen door headed for Little Dink's house. I saw Little Dink, Stump, and a couple of other neighborhood kids outside Little Dink's kitchen door.

"Guess what, guess what. You are never going to guess what I am going to get this afternoon," I announced.

They all had a puzzled look on their faces, and their guesses ranged from BB guns, to bicycles, to shotguns.

"Mama is going to buy me a go-cart, and all of you will get to ride it," I cheerfully stammered.

I was so excited, I could hardly contain myself. I turned around and ran home. It wasn't ten minutes later that Little Dink, Stump, and two others joined me on the front stoop of our house. Mama pulled out of the yard in her car, on her way to pick up my go-cart. In the meantime, several other kids had joined us and were caught up in my excitement. As I look back on this time now, I'm not so sure I would have shared in the excitement for someone else's pleasure. I probably would have been jealous, but here they sat anxious for my mother's return.

There were a couple of neighborhood girls who came over to satisfy their curiosity. Perhaps, they were there to convince me of their sudden friendship. Either way, to have girls around was always funny and weird.

"Will, you are the luckiest guy I know, of all people you are getting a go-cart. *Wow*, how lucky can someone be," Stump sang out. "Who's going to be the first one to ride it?" he asked cheerfully as he scooted even closer to my side.

"I am," I replied loudly. "Who else? Maybe you can tomorrow," I joked.

We must have sat on the grassy bank in our yard for an hour. We stared at the bottom of Spring Street where we knew she would eventually turn in on her way home.

"There she is, Will, here comes your mom," Wart shouted.

That old Chevy wagon crept ever so slowly up the hill. Why so slow? Why so deliberate? I was about to find out. Mama looked straight ahead when she passed us as she began to turn in to our side yard driveway. I didn't notice any steering wheel or any other parts of a go-cart from our angle. She parked the car and opened the door as she smiled at me.

"I am so sorry, son, I am so sorry…there is no go-cart," she said. "Come on in the house and let me explain."

I don't remember if I looked at my friends when I heard the news. I assumed they shared in my disappointment. Some knew how I felt and found their way home. I went to the living room and sat down to wait and wonder what Mama was about to tell me.

"I apologize for getting your hopes up. I should have tried to buy the go-cart before I told you about my plan, but I was excited even more than you," she said. "The go-cart was just too fast and I didn't want you to possibly injure yourself or others. The man who owns the go-cart had put a motorcycle engine on it, and the engine was just too powerful.

I couldn't take the chance of possibly losing you on such a dangerous machine."

Mama started to cry. I started to cry because of her. I never wanted to see my mother that upset ever. Nothing in this world was worth it, especially a go-cart. One of the most important things I learned that day was that Mama made an important decision, one that possibly saved my life or someone else's.

Chapter 13
Dead Man's Curve

Screech, blam, kawhump, the worst sounds imaginable on a hot Saturday afternoon in the village. There were six of us MilliKids in the middle of Spring Street playing baseball when we heard these awful, yet telling, sounds from a few blocks away. The first thing we did was turn our attention to the bottom of the hill to see if any birds were surfing on the power lines.

Noises such as these meant only two possibilities; first, there was a car wreck at the intersection of Quarry Street and Cornelia Highway, or there was a wreck at the intersection of East Main Street and Cornelia Highway. Either way, someone was in trouble, and we wanted to confirm it before we called an ambulance. Our first clue was to look at the power lines on the utility poles located next to the highway at the bottom of the hill. We could usually tell by the rippling of those lines the severity of the crash, and the direction of the ripples told us which end of the highway the wreck occurred.

"It's a big one!" Stump shouted, and we took off in a full run.

"Call an ambulance Mama, there's another wreck," I yelled.

When we reached the highway, we looked toward the direction where the ripples in the power lines had started. There was a car flipped on its side between the utility pole and the fence in front of the mill. We could see the smoke as it billowed from under the car, and we proceeded with caution to Dead Man's Curve. It was called that because of the many car wrecks and fatalities that occurred there over the years. We could already hear the sirens in the distance and a police vehicle was already on scene.

Just eight years earlier, two older MilliKids were killed in a horrible crash at the same location. There were five boys in one car as it returned from Gainesville when the driver lost control and wrapped his car around the utility pole. Two New Holland teens were instantly killed and one other injured for life, crushed legs and damaged spine.

"The police are already here," I said. "That was quick!"

As the six of us neared the accident, we could hear the screams, moans, and groans of the passengers. It appeared to be two men and two women in the car. One woman was not moving.

"Stay back, boys, this is not for you, you hear me? Stay clear I said!" commanded the police officer.

"There's one still pinned inside the vehicle," the officer said. "We'll have to roll the vehicle over to free him."

There were about five or six other men on the scene and, at the request of the officer, they worked together to upright the car to free the trapped man inside. They did, but the man was dead. We heard the ambulance attendant say the words..."this one's gone."

It frightened us. None of us had ever seen a dead person except at a funeral.

We could overhear the officer tell how he chased them from the city limits of Gainesville because of their excessive speed. His exact words were...

"They wouldn't stop so I gave chase. About a half mile back they almost lost control but continued their course. My lights flashed, but the siren didn't work. I don't know if they knew I was behind them or not."

The smell of alcohol was everywhere. Obviously, they were drunk and now one of them was dead. We were visibly shaken and scared at the same time. It left an emotional scar on me that I carry today.

My brother was a "hot-rodder" of sorts; I can thank him and this accident, plus several other accidents we witnessed, for keeping me away from fast cars. The only one of us that didn't learn a lesson from this incident was Wart. He had several wrecks in his youth due to carelessness and disregard, but he is still alive today by the grace of God.

"I'm going home," I said. "See you guys tomorrow."

It was a long walk home, and Little Dink and Stump joined me. Wart stayed because his dad had arrived.

"That's a dangerous curve," Little Dink said. "How many wrecks have we seen here?"

"Two or three," Stump answered.

The Hughes family, who lived on Quarry Street just a couple of houses away from the highway, actually found it amusing and entertaining to sit on their front porch every weekend and wait for a wreck to happen. They were seldom disappointed. Today was no different, they were gathered on the bank in front of the church, taking it all in. To wait for something this terrible to happen doesn't make sense to me.

Little Dink, Stump, and I made a vow on our way home to stay away from fast cars and booze.

I took the vow seriously. I'm not sure about Little Dink and Stump. Honestly, I forgot about the vow, but the impressions these accidents and other incidents in my life that involved fast cars and alcohol have stayed with me. I'm no saint, but I'm not a drunk or hot-rodder either.

Mama waited on the front porch…"Well, how bad was it?" she asked.

"Three people seriously injured and one dead," I said. I didn't know how to soften it.

"Anybody we know?"

"No ma'am."

Mama was quite upset.

"What's wrong, Mama?" I asked. "We don't know any of them."

"Son, there are two other mothers within earshot of us right now that lost their sons eight years ago in that same curve. I don't want to know their pain," she said. "Your brother drives too fast, and I'm afraid I'm going to join them if he doesn't slow down."

I hugged her, and she held me close and tight. I could hear and feel her sobs. I never wanted to see my mother upset like that again, and that's when I promised myself to always drive carefully.

Later on that week, Daddy and I were on our way to the grocery store. As we passed Dead Man's Curve, a car was headed straight at us on our side of the road. The driver had passed a car then had to swerve back into his lane, and even leave the road to avoid a collision with us. My heart stopped as I turned in my seat and watched what I thought was one of the most amazing things I had ever seen. The driver of the car maneuvered it so well that when he left the road he had to go between the utility pole and the mill fence, barely a car's width distance from the pole.

I turned around, looked at Daddy, but couldn't say a word. I was terrified, shocked, scared, and somewhat proud that an accident didn't happen. The driver was my brother, Butter. He was coming home from work for lunch—he must have been really hungry.

Daddy never said a word; he puffed on his cigar and continued on to Kroger's. We returned home about an hour later. Whether he said anything to my mother or my brother, I don't know.

But I do know this, I don't remember a time when my daddy drove faster than forty-five miles an hour. Everybody in the village knew he was slow. He didn't drink alcohol either, just smoked cigars. I have always wondered if something happened early in his life to cause him to take it slow. Probably not, more likely he never had a car that would run faster than forty-five.

"Hey Will, can you come over?" Little Dink asked. "I want to show you something."

"Let me finish dinner, and I'll be right there."

I gulped down what was left and scooted over to Little Dink's house.

"You're not going to believe this after all we have seen in the last few weeks, come here," he said as he opened the car house door. People in the village kept their cars either on the street or in car houses, similar to a garage.

Inside was his brother's car. He had crashed it the night before, and it was nearly destroyed. Sal, Little Dink's brother, drove home from college and wrecked it, flipped it over, but survived.

"He's inside, but nobody can visit him. He's injured and in a bad mood," Little Dink said.

I wanted to tell him about my brother's close call, but I couldn't.

"Little Dink, we made a promise to each other, remember?" I asked.

"I remember. Don't worry, when you see Sal's face, just another reminder to be careful."

I discovered later my brother kept a bottle of booze in his car. It was shortly after his near accident that he was married. That's when he slowed down somewhat, but I'll never forget that accident he almost caused and what it would have done to Mama. Daddy must have gotten his attention somehow. In a way, I can thank my brother and Dink's brother for making sure I avoided fast cars.

Chapter 14

Wheels

The sidewalks of the village were often covered with kids in wagons or on bikes. Everyone wanted to *ride*, and one of the most exciting modes of travel was on a *homemade* wagon. Every wagon was primitive—simply, a long board, usually two inches by six inches and least four feet long. It had a smaller board to serve as the front axle with either a nail driven through the main board and bent underneath to allow the cross member to swivel, or, if you were fortunate, you had a bolt, washers, and a nut to serve the same purpose.

It had a similar board on the rear that was fixed, usually nails to secure this board to the main board. We inherited axles from the earlier generation of MilliKids, and we sawed the front and rear boards to accommodate the length of the axles. Axles were usually fixed to the boards by nails that were hammered over to allow the axle to rotate during movement.

Wheels, now, were a separate and entirely different entity. Most of us MilliKids took the wheels off a dilapidated metal wagon. Some of our fathers, however, would find some wheels in the mill from cloth carts or, if we were really lucky, wheels from a steel frame that transported heavier equipment. These wheels usually had ball bearings in them, which made them roll truer and certainly faster. Axles generally had a hole through each end to allow for a cotter pin, or nail in our case, to hold the wheel in place. Coca-Cola crates were used for seating by simply taking off one side and nailing the crate to the main board.

We guided, steered, and controlled these vehicles with our feet placed on the front board and, depending on which way we wanted to turn, let up with one foot as we pressed forward with the other. These wagons lasted as long as the wheels held up (unless they were steel wheels), or until one of the boards split from overuse or abuse. Either way, we wore the streets and sidewalks out.

"What in the world is that?" Little Dink anxiously asked one day.

"I have never seen such," I remarked.

"That family has just about everything," Stump chimed in.

Zee, zee, zee.

"What a sound," I said. "Where in the world did they get that contraption?"

"Jules is flying; that's the fastest wagon I have ever seen," said Wart. "Let's go check it out."

We ran across Spring Street to the sidewalk next to the gym. Not only was this the fastest wagon any of us had ever seen, it was an awesome sight. You could tell it was well built and had been painted, no less.

"Jules, where did you get this wagon?" I asked. "I have never seen anything like it."

"Papa and I built it. It's the fastest wagon in New Holland," he said.

Jules' family and his grandparents lived below Miss Icie's. There were five children, Jules, a brother named Gibson, his sister, and two much younger brothers. Gibson was the oldest, but Jules spent much more time with us than he did.

"How do you like my steering wheel?" Jules asked.

His Papa Dan had used a broomstick for a steering column and rope that was attached to each side of the front board. He then wound the rope around the broomstick from bottom to nearly the top where another wheel was used for a steering device. It was cool and we were envious. As you turned the steering wheel the rope would unwind or wind according to the direction you turned it, which also governed the direction of the front end. Not only that, but

Papa Dan had also made a handbrake that created friction against the rear wheel when slowed or stopped as necessary.

"Can I try it?" I asked. "I promise not to damage anything."

"Sure, go ahead, but be careful." Jules said.

"This is amazing and so much faster," I said with a hint of envy.

I began to think of a way to make mine as fast or faster. I went home and went to work, only to quickly discover that my talents and abilities, mechanically speaking, were nonexistent. I went inside to ask Daddy and brother for help, but was predictably ignored. I was on my own. I tried and tried, even went back to get another eye view of Jules' contraption, but that didn't help.

"You want to race?" Gibson challenged. "There's no way you can outrun Jules."

It was worth a try, but I was going to let Wart ride my wagon. He was much lighter, and I really didn't want to lose to either one of those boys. Wart agreed. The sidewalk wasn't big enough for two wagons so Jules was on one side of Spring Street while Wart and I were on the other. We decided on a stopping point. For Jules, he could turn onto the adjoining sidewalk to slow down, but Wart had to swerve in to Papa Dan's yard.

"Come on, come on, come on," Jules yelled. "Let's get this show on the road."

Both boys pretended they had motors, so they provided the sounds of two engines as they revved up for battle. By this time, we had an audience gathered: Papa Dan, his wife, Jules' sister, and Little Dink and Stump. I was the starter.

"Is everyone ready?" I asked. "Start your engines."

They did, you could hear both of them from the next block over.

"When I drop my raised hand you can take off." I said.

I slowly raised my hand but then quickly dropped it trying to catch Jules off guard. I didn't. They're off.

It was almost as if Jules had an engine. He flew down the sidewalk and made the turn with ease onto the adjacent walkway. Wart, on the other hand (and with much disappointment), went all of twenty feet before a rear wheel came off.

"What in the world, what in the world!" Wart screamed.

Not only did the wheel come off, but then it started to roll on its own toward the bottom of the hill in the middle of the street headed toward traffic on Highway 23. As we watched the wheel, Wart flipped out into the street himself, and the wagon (what was left of it) landed on top of him. He had a few choice words for me and took off home, angry and crying. All I could do was hope that wheel made it across the highway without crashing into an oncoming car, perhaps causing a wreck. I was embarrassed. Everyone laughed but me. The wheel did make it across the highway and came to rest against the store. No harm done except to my ego — and Wart's butt.

It was time to take my medicine, to face the taunts, but they didn't come. As a matter of fact, I noticed Jules as he walked toward the bottom of the hill where my wheel had come to rest. He crossed the highway, retrieved the wheel, and returned it to me.

"Let's fix your wagon so we can have a real race," Jules said.

That was probably the first time Jules and I ever did anything together — he became a friend that day. His offer to help me repair my wagon gave me reason to smile. I have to admit, Jules was a couple of years younger, but he was also wiser in many ways. He had a natural sense for things, and I believe that was what helped him become successful later in life.

"Okay, that should do it," Jules remarked as we put the finishing touches on my wagon.

"Let's give it another shot while no one is around," he said.

Jules took his wagon across the street again and I stayed on the sidewalk nearest Miss Icie's.

"You say when, Will."

"Now," I said.

As I looked over to check on his progress he had already reached the finish line and was skirting up the adjoining sidewalk. As for me, I coasted to rest in Papa Dan's yard, but somehow I was not as disappointed. We looked at each other and laughed.

"Here, you come race my wagon, and I'll race yours," Jules offered.

"I don't believe there will be any difference," I said. "Yours is much faster, no matter who drives it."

Wart ventured back over after he gained some composure, and Jules even let him ride his wagon.

Papa Dan had to be a terrific grandfather. As I look back on those years, I can appreciate that family even more. I know they had their own problems like any other, but Papa Dan seemed to always be around, even when the two younger brothers came along. A generation seemed to separate the three older children from the two younger, but their family was close, and I believe Papa Dan had a lot to do with it.

Chapter 15
Listen and Learn

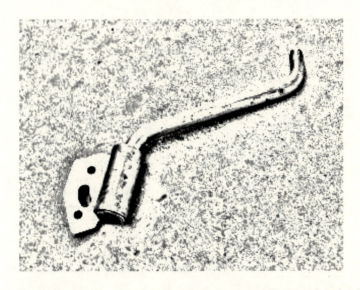

Kickstands were for *sissies*. Boys in the village either laid their bikes on the ground or leaned them against something, but never used a kickstand. Most of us removed the stand because it looked like it didn't belong. Anyway, all I had left one morning as a reminder of the bike I owned the day before was its' kickstand. It was lying on the porch where I put it, but my bike was gone.

"Come on, Will, let's go the ballpark; we've got a game with Branch Street," yelled Little Dink.

I just watched him as he rode by on his bicycle. I didn't say a word. He got about half way down Spring Street and turned to see if I followed him. He noticed that I remained on my front porch then slammed on his brakes as he slid and turned so he could face me.

"Are you coming or not?" he asked.

I shook my head no and sat down on the top step.

"What is wrong with you? You always want to play baseball!" he exclaimed.

"Someone stole my bicycle, and I don't feel like doing anything," I said.

"Your bike was stolen?"

"Yep!"

"Do you know who took it?"

"No!"

"Where did you leave it last?"

I pointed to a spot in my front yard where I always parked it, even though I was told over and over never to leave it where someone may take it. But did I listen?

"I'll be back after a while, and we can look for it then, okay?" he asked. "I'll ask Stump and Wart to help. Surely, we'll find it."

I went back inside the house and sat on the sofa in front of the TV. Mama was on her way from upstairs and noticed my despair.

"What's the matter, son?" she asked.

"Someone stole my bike, just like you and Daddy warned." I said. "It's hard to believe that a person in this neighborhood would take something that belonged to somebody else."

"We tried to warn you, but you wouldn't listen," Mama replied. "Your brother will be up in a few minutes, and he can go with you and look for it. Maybe whoever took it just rode it so far and dumped it close by."

I didn't get my hopes up, and I didn't look forward to my brother, Butter, helping me find it either. All he was going to do was make fun of me and kid me about it.

I was on the front porch swing when Butter came to the door with a huge grin on his face...

"I knew it, I just knew it. You didn't listen did you?" he snickered.

"I'll help you look for it, but go around to the basement gate and get the washtub for Mama. She's washing Skipper today," he said.

Skipper was Mama's pet Chihuahua who had needed a bath for months. You could smell him two blocks away. I walked around to the back of the house and opened the basement gate where Mama kept the washtub.

"Oh my gosh, oh my gosh!" I yelled. "Here's my bike, here's my bike Mama...Butter!"

I was thrilled for a moment, and then I thought, *Why was my bike in the basement*? Mama and Butter had followed me around to the rear of the house and enjoyed my surprise.

"Let this be a lesson to you. I had Butter bring your bike here to get your attention. Do not leave it outside inviting someone to steal it, okay?" Mama scowled.

"Yes, ma'am, I promise. I will never leave it on the front yard ever again," I said.

I was in a hurry, the game had probably started without me. All I needed was my glove. I flew down to the ballpark and arrived just in time.

"Where did you find it?" Little Dink asked.

"Mama and Butter played a trick on me. They had warned me for weeks to not leave it out front at night. I left it there last night, and Butter put it in the basement to teach me a lesson. Let's play ball!" I said cheerfully.

It was midmorning, already hot and humid, so we ended the game shortly before lunch. Little Dink, Stump, Wart, and I walked our bikes back up the hill to the top of Spring Street and went to my house for some cold water.

I was happy that my bike wasn't stolen. I was going to tie it to the porch rails at night just to be safe. I did just that for about a week. Then one evening as I returned from Little Dink's and without thinking about it, left my bike in the yard and went inside the house. Even though I had probably finished with it for the day, I decided to wait until later to secure it to the porch. I forgot. When I awoke the next morning and realized what I failed to do the night before, I rushed to the front door to make sure my bike was still there. It wasn't. I crept into the kitchen where Mama and Daddy were eating breakfast and asked…

"Mama, did you and Butter play a trick on me again?" I gently asked.

They looked at each other and with all seriousness, both shook their heads no. I raced upstairs to my brother's bed, and he also said he had nothing to do with it this time. Indeed, my bicycle had been stolen.

Three or four days went by. My friends and I had spent quite a bit of time as we looked for it, but to no avail. The bike was gone forever. It's real this time, and it became one of the saddest periods of my life.

I had a sneaky suspicion who stole it. An older, meaner kid in the neighborhood we called Snort. He was always in trouble and a bully on top of that. It all made sense, but how could I prove it? Why did I believe it to be him?

Three weeks earlier, I was in the backyard playing basketball by myself. I always had a ball and hoop and spent hour upon hour upon hour shooting baskets, especially when I couldn't get into the gym. This one particular morning Snort came into my backyard, took the ball away, and taunted me with it. Fortunately, Butter had watched the whole episode from the kitchen window. I could hear the screen door slam shut, and I mean hard. I looked around, and here came Butter.

"This is my brother, this is his backyard, this is his basketball, this is his hoop, and I am his brother. Now get your butt out of here and don't ever come back," Butter demanded.

Snort took off, and I was so tickled I started to laugh in relief. My brother tossed me the ball and said...

"If he ever bothers you again, let me know."

The irony was how my brother had tortured me most of my life, like big brothers do, but on more than one occasion had come to my rescue to scare away the neighborhood bullies.

About a week had gone by when another older neighborhood friend met me at the gym and told me he knew who stole my bike because he was with him. He said it was Snort, and he knew exactly where my bike was — in the lake behind the mill.

"Will, as we walked down the sidewalk in front of your house, he noticed your bike and remarked how he was going to get even with you for what your brother had done. He picked up your bike and began to ride it down the hill. I tried to get him to stop, but I was afraid of him and didn't have the courage to tell you until now. We crossed the highway, and he rode it around to the rear of the mill where he pushed it off the dock into the lake. I am so sorry Will."

I never told anyone about this, not even my brother. What good would it do? Snort was an unhappy person, and I decided to live with the fact that his life didn't need to get worse because of me. Thirty-five years passed before I saw him again.

It was on the old ball field when our paths crossed. As I hit golf balls, he happened to walk by and stopped to watch. Our eyes met. I felt sorry for him. I had often heard he had a horrible life, and I wasn't about to make it worse. I kept my mouth shut and nodded to him as if to say, "It's okay Snort, I forgive you." He turned and walked away. What was even more remarkable was that we stood near the lake where my bicycle still lay, wet and rusty after all those years.

Chapter 16
Waterless Chasm

We were the MilliKids and we knew we were safe from most of the problems of the world. We always seemed to have what we needed to survive and, more importantly, we knew how to have fun. Yes, you could probably declare that what we had was a "gang," not in the same sense as most of today's gangs, but nevertheless, a gang. Usually gangs have hideouts or places to congregate and plan each night's activities. Today's definition of a gang such as ours could be more accurately described by using the word "crew." The main difference between a crew and a gang is the sound of the name. Gang typically implied something a little wiser and somewhat tougher. Therefore, we will use the word crew for our tight, close-knit, passive, somewhat pitiful group.

MilliKids spent most of every day with each other. The worst criminal act the crew ever committed was to sneak into

Mr. Coker's backyard at night and help ourselves to his grapes, or venture to Mr. Cody's apple trees, or perhaps to invade Mr. Ball's terrace and help ourselves to his turnips. *Turnips?* Yep, turnips. Can't explain why, but we loved turnips, especially when they were still in the ground. Ordinarily, we wouldn't dare think to take something from someone without permission but this was a challenge, and we never got caught. Well almost. Then we would gather together at our refuge, the Gym, to enjoy the spoils of our efforts.

The crew actually performed some noble deeds for special neighbors. We cut grass, trimmed hedges, and swept front porches and expected nothing in return. But we always gathered in front of the gym at nightfall, especially after Miss Icie had retired for the evening.

The gym was a warm harbor of sorts, and a place of comfort and safety that provided us endless hours of fun and sometimes fright. I call it a refuge because it was always there, seemingly impenetrable, and it was ours, whether the mill (who built it in 1921) or, later on, the local board of education (which took it over in the early 60s) knew it or not. It was *the gym,* and that's where the MilliKids attempted to grow up.

On this particularly warm, breezy night, not unlike most others, we sensed something suspicious and scary in the air. We didn't know for sure what to expect, but our senses told us this night was going to be different. The gym had been condemned for public use several years before—a safety hazard they said. We knew how to gracefully sneak in, find, and often repair light switches, fuse boxes, or even replace light bulbs, if necessary, to have our night of fun.

We were forbidden to be in the gym without Mr. Pete's permission. Mr. Pete was its caretaker. He wasn't always available, so we took it upon ourselves to sneak into this massive structure of hardwood floors and play basketball. That was our intention anyway, the two-lane bowling alley, in the catacombs of the Gym, and the steam-heated swimming pool had been declared irreparable for years.

Since its inception in the 1920s, the gym had been the focal point of the mill village. It became an expensive and ill-kept eyesore as the 60s approached. But for us kids, it was our sanctuary, our haven, our daily and nightly place to retreat. As mentioned earlier, the gym was built in 1921 by the Pacolet Company, which had also built the cotton mill, our duplex homes, churches, and school. Even though it had four levels of recreational pleasure and leisure within its brick walls, it was now a foreboding and somewhat eerie place to visit, especially at night. But little did we know that this would be a night to remember. Our mission this evening was to play basketball.

Stump was always our go-to guy when we needed something done in the dark. He pretended not to be afraid, but I knew him well enough to know that he only needed an audience to carry out the questionable deed none of the rest of us wanted to do.

"Hey Stump, come on over here. I'll help you remove the window," Little Dink urged.

I admit, we did break a window to make the breaking and entering a little easier on us, but what we had done was to put in a replacement window and let it appear to be repaired. In fact, it just sat in the slots of the slats and was easily removed when necessary.

The scary part was that the window was on the same level as the swimming pool, which was below ground level, and it was always dark and dreary down there. But Stump removed the temporary pane, slipped through the hole, found a foot support on a barrel we kept next to the pool and eased himself into the gym where he would go to the nearest door, unlock it, and let us in.

"Shuh, shuh," Stump whispered as he stalled halfway through the open pane, "there's somebody in here."

"Come on, Stump, enough's enough, just get the door open?" Little Dink snapped.

We thought he was kidding, but when I poked my head through the opening I could hear voices and laughter coming from the girls' dressing room. We helped each other in, tiptoed across the tiled floor, and hoisted ourselves up the wall to the balcony where spectators once sat. We grouped ourselves on the balcony and began to eavesdrop on our uninvited, yet entertaining guests. Entertaining because we could tell from the commotion somebody was up to no good. We were always braver as a crew because none of us would even think about going inside this "graveyard" of memories alone.

We had no sooner settled in on the balcony area when one of the men ran, laughed, and hopped out of the dressing room butt naked. He dove horizontally into the shallow end of the waterless chasm of rock. Waterless, yes, it had been empty for years. It seemed like minutes before we heard the contact he made with his chin, his chest, and his thighs. The scrape of skin to stone for several feet was jaw-dropping and breath-catching. Before we could react...

"Good goshamighty..." Little Dink started to blurt, but I quickly covered his mouth. Another man burst through the dressing room door and jumped feet first into the same area.

Thud, kathud, whump, kafumph...Yelps and the foulest language imaginable filled the pool area. Next came moans and groans and subtle little whimpering gasps, followed by the monotonous tones of obvious pain.

We lay low, not one word was uttered. We didn't know whether to laugh, cry out for help, or call for an ambulance. We quickly decided not to give away our presence or offer assistance to two naked, skinned, and drunken men.

"Come on guys, let's get out of here now. We'll see them when they leave." I whispered.

"Will, let's help...never mind, we don't need to do that; let's get the heck out of here before they see us," Wart said as we quickly bolted through the front door.

Outside, we collected ourselves behind the big rock that was always present in front of the gym. There was an old Ford pickup on the street up a little ways from the gym.

It wasn't too long before two men, one kind of familiar, the other not, eased awkwardly, and I mean *awkwardly*, out the door and, toward the truck. We could hear their mutters while they adjusted their clothing. We started to giggle, and as soon as the truck was out of sight, we laughed until we cried.

"Come on, let's see how far we can follow the truck and maybe discover who those men are," Stump said.

Myrtle Drive snaked up and around the gym, so we headed the opposite way knowing they had to come back down Spring Street or Highland Avenue. We had gotten no further than halfway up Spring when we noticed a block over under the street light, the truck pulling to a stop. We sneaked behind Miss Icie's over the terrace and into the gulch that runs between the houses on Carolina and Spring streets. As we crept up besides Mr. Collin's house, we got a good look at one of the victims. At first we thought it was one of our neighbors we call Wormy, but a closer look revealed his unmistakable identity. We were still giddy, but were shocked to discover it was one of our friend's dads. When we thought we couldn't laugh anymore, we did, uncontrollably. We only stopped, when the truth hit us.

"I'm getting out of here," said Little Dink.

"See you later," echoed Stump as he disappeared into the darkness.

"It's way past my bedtime," said Wart, as he sneaked in the side door of his house.

It's not important whose father it was. As far as I know, nothing has ever been mentioned about that night. Friendships are sacred, so is a person's integrity.

Chapter 17
Crocker Gator

The Crocker family lived around the corner from us on Highland Avenue. There was Ole Man Crocker, we called him Half-Step because he had only half of a foot. He somehow let it slip under his push mower one summer and nearly cut his foot off. They had a steep bank in front of their house and it must have been almost impossible to cut. Anyway, he attempted to let the mower slide down the hill almost to the street when he slipped and his foot became lodged under the mower...an operation later...and he is known as Half-Step. He lived there with his wife and two teenage daughters.

Not many families in the mill village took vacations because they couldn't afford it. The families that could, never went very far or stayed gone long, but the Crockers liked to visit Florida. Going to Florida was just a dream for Little Dink, Wart, and me. Our summer vacations were spent mainly on the streets, backyards, and in the New Holland Gym. Stump took trips with his family occasionally, but we never knew where he went, or if he told us we didn't believe him. We just knew he was gone for a few days. It was kind of nice not having him around all the time.

This summer afternoon, there were six of us playing baseball on Spring Street out in front of the church. It was at the top of the hill so when a car turned on to Spring Street from the main highway, about 130 yards away, we had plenty of time to move.

It was Little Dink's turn at bat, and we used the manhole cover located at the crest of Spring Street for home plate.

"Will, are you going to throw the ball or not?" Little Dink snapped. "We don't have all day."

I was looking past him to the bottom of the hill when I noticed the Crocker family as they turned onto Spring.

"Hold your horses, Little Dink, here come the Crockers." I said. "It's going to take a couple of minutes for them to get here; you know how slow Ole Man Crocker is with a half foot and all."

As they went by Mrs. Crocker waved at us, but the old man never acknowledged our existence. They proceeded to turn down Highland and continue home. We continued to play, but about thirty minutes later one of the Crocker girls came out to where we were and said…

"Do you boys want to see something interesting and scary? We just returned from our trip to Florida and brought an alligator home with us. Come on if you want to see it," she said.

"An alligator, in New Holland," Stump exclaimed, "she's pulling our legs."

"Let's go find out," I said.

We started running down Highland to satisfy our curiosity. As we climbed the hill to their side porch, we could tell they already had a big wash tub in the yard with a hose pipe filling it with water.

"Whoa, whoa, whoa, boys, y'all just hang on for a second," Ole Man Crocker ordered, "this thing is dangerous and wild."

We came to a sliding halt and tried to peer over the side of the wash tub from about twenty feet away.

"All right, come on over, but be careful, this thing might jump out and have one of you for supper," the old man said.

All of us crept slowly and quietly to the side of the wash tub and looked in. Sure enough, there was an alligator, but he was only about five or six inches long. The Crockers started to laugh at us. We had never seen anything like this before, especially in real life. They told us they had bought the alligator for two dollars in Florida.

We hung around for a couple of minutes. I believed the Crockers had had enough fun with us for the moment. We hurried back to Spring Street to finish our game.

"An alligator in New Holland, boy, now that's something," Wart said, "I wonder what they are going to name it?"

"I wonder what they are going to feed it!" Stump thought out loud.

"It'll probably eat whatever it wants," I said. "Now let's play ball."

A couple of weeks passed by and one afternoon as we were gathered on the steps of the church, the other Crocker daughter came and asked if we wanted to see the alligator again.

"Sure," we all said in unison.

"Come on then."

"What's its name? Have you named it yet?" Little Dink asked.

"Oh yes, his name is Roebuck. We thought of that when we were at Sears and Roebuck looking for a bigger wash tub. He outgrew the other one," she continued.

"Outgrew it," I said, "you've got to be kidding."

They had moved Roebuck to an area in the backyard inside a chicken wire fence and in to a much bigger wash tub. Before we could get closer we could actually hear him as he moved around in it.

"Now be careful, boys, he's pretty active, and I don't want you to excite him," Mrs. Crocker said as she stood on her back porch.

He had grown so much. He was at least a foot and a half long and banged the sides of the wash tub with authority. He was, indeed, quite active even in the tub, which was also covered with a piece of wood to protect onlookers and to keep him in check.

It occurred to me, *What would they put him in next?*

All of us MilliKids were glad he wasn't our responsibility.

Weeks passed, and we had heard a few stories about Roebuck getting out, but we also heard that the backyard was now enclosed high enough to offer him freedom to roam.

Several of us were on our bikes one day when we noticed the Crockers' car. We watched them as they turned onto Highland and proceeded home. As we sat on the bank in my front yard we heard this thunderous eruption of screams and yells. Quickly, we raced on our bikes to where the noise came from. Sure enough, from the Crocker house. When they returned from town, they had checked on Roebuck and discovered he was *gone*. The whole family was frantic, even the old man was beside himself hobbling around on a foot and a half.

We all chipped in to investigate his escape. There was a hole under one end of the chicken wire fence where he had dug through. The Crockers, us, and a few other neighbors began to scour the neighbor's yards. We found no evidence of his departure. Even the continued search the next day brought no results. Roebuck had disappeared. Months went by before he even became part of any of our conversations.

In the village we had what was called "the pasture," where, at one time, some of the families in New Holland raised pigs, chickens, and a few cows. At one end of the pasture was a swampy area, so we decided that Roebuck had found a new home there. We didn't look for him any longer, but a couple of mysterious happenings began to occur. We knew of two or three neighbors' cats and dogs that had ventured into the pasture and came back mangled and mauled. This included my mother's dog, Skipper. One day, he just showed up at the side door all shriveled and bloody. Something had definitely gotten hold of him. Our neighbors up the street, the Buffingtons, mentioned that they had a cat vanish. This led to a lot of speculation about the swamp area and the possibility that Roebuck was a terror to any animals that visited that part of the pasture. So we stayed clear.

There were many times, especially in summer, that the MilliKids would hike through the pasture to play games or whatever, but were always careful to stay away from the swampy end. It was also reported that a worker in the mill had spotted an alligator near the lake located behind the mill, but proof was never provided. Roebuck had vanished, and he has not been seen since. It is not known for sure what the lifespan of an alligator is, but some have lived past fifty years, which means that Roebuck could still be alive today.

Who really knows what happened to him? Did someone take him to a refuge of some sort, or did someone possibly kill Roebuck? We're not sure, but one thing is for certain, Roebuck gave us several days of excitement. There have

Crocker Gator

been reports since the 1960s of alligator sightings in Hall County so the possibility of his existence is real. One thing has changed. You can't go to Florida and buy an alligator for two dollars anymore. Come to think of it, who would want a pet like that anyway? Only the Crockers. Those girls were always wanting attention, and they got plenty that summer.

Chapter 18
Shock and Riles

Heroes were mostly sports figures during the 50s and 60s. Babe Ruth, Mickey Mantle, Johnny Unitas, and Wilt Chamberlain were just a few of the many men we idolized when we were young. However, in our little village we had some iconic figures of our own. Even though I was pretty close in age to these two young men, they still loomed large in our minds.

Shock could do just about anything sports-wise. He was much better than average in basketball and baseball. He thought he had a way with the girls, and he did, but what I remember most is how he treated my friends and me. He never looked down on us. He would always cut up and include us when he could, especially when teams were chosen for either baseball or basketball. He always encouraged and supported us younger kids. Shock remained that way until he passed away while playing golf a few years ago. But, for the most part, of those fifty years I knew him, I was glad to call him a friend.

Riles, an above average athlete in his own rights, wasn't as friendly to us. He often looked over and beyond my friends and me, but he was still someone I always admired and respected. Later on, he became an encourager and even a friend. We played on the same basketball team for a short time and that is where he rose, in my estimation, to a trusted friend.

Little Dink and I were in Stump's backyard one afternoon, just tossing a football around, when we were suddenly joined by Riles and one of his cousins, who lived on Victor Street located below Stump's house.

"Give me that ball, Stump!" Riles demanded as he held out his hands anticipating a pass from Stump.

"Oh yeah, yeah, here. Riles, let me hit you with a pass," Stump responded as he threw the ball five yards short of where Riles stood.

"What was that?" Riles' cousin exclaimed as he mocked the way Stump had thrown the ball.

"Let us show you boys how it's done."

Little Dink and I stepped aside. I waited anxiously for a pass to be thrown my way. Stump's brother, Ernie, came out on his back-porch and stood there to watch. He wanted his presence known. Ernie was huge and very protective of Stump. He was a couple of years older than Riles and his cousin. While they all played on the same high school football team, it was clear that Ernie had little time for either under these circumstances.

"Hey Ernie," Riles spoke up, trying to soften his presence in Ernie's backyard, "We're just playing around, no harm done."

"Oh, I'm sure there won't be any harm done," Ernie responded as he turned and went back into his house.

His short-lived presence was enough security for us. It let Riles and his cousin know that he was close by in case he was needed.

"I'll get my own brother if I have to," Little Dink snorted.

His brother was also a high school athlete (a terrific one at that) and was a pretty big guy as well. He was also several years older than Riles, his cousin, and Ernie.

"I would go get my older brother, Butter, but he might be in the middle of a sandwich," If I disturbed his eating, I was afraid I would be the recipient of his wrath. "No, I'll let him be, he would probably take sides against me anyway," I said to Stump.

My older brother had many gifts, talents, and abilities, but an athlete he wasn't. He did offer a level of protection over me that I knew was always there if I needed it. I did later on, but not today. I let him enjoy his sandwich.

"I'll go get Shock, and we can divide up teams to play your guys," I blurted, trying to act tough.

I didn't want to play football with them, but Ernie's presence had made us a little over confident and zealous in our efforts to speak up and talk back to these two.

"Go ahead, Will, see if you can find some real men to take us on," Riles responded.

What was I to do now? I had opened my mouth when usually I kept it closed, but I had to respond somehow. I turned and ran toward Shock's house, which was just a few blocks away. He and his brother, Lewis, were outside with some other kids playing basketball at the "carhouse." (The carhouse was the village's version of a garage, except it was completely detached from the house.) Little Dink and Stump were with me as I informed Shock, Lewis, and the other kids of Riles' challenge.

"You go tell him that we will meet his crew in the gym at two o'clock if he wants a game, otherwise he's just blowing smoke like usual," Shock replied.

"You tell him Lewis said to bring it on," Lewis snapped.

Lewis had this unique ability to get his two cents in even when it didn't matter. He was especially bold at doing this when his big brother was around to look out for him. He still owns this unique ability today, but again, I am glad to call him friend.

We took off and soon located Riles, his cousin, and a few more wannabes down on Victor Street. It was almost like they had prepared for a gang fight except this fight would involve a ball of some kind, and fisticuffs were never part of the plan.

"We've got our team," I urged, "but they want to play basketball in the gym at two o'clock."

"Oh yeah, that's right, those are the sissies from Quarry Street; they're not men enough to play football," Riles' cousin quipped.

"We'll be there at two o'clock, and they better not be late," Riles warned.

It was two o'clock and there were ten of us waiting outside the gym doors for this "Battle of the Blocks" to take place.

"Anybody got the keys to the gym?" Shock asked.

"Mr. Pete is working, so we will have to slip in through one of the windows," Riles responded.

Everyone knew a way to get in the gym if the keys were not available. A broken or loose window or a gimpy door was always ready to be compromised.

"Come on, I'll show you the easiest way to get in," I offered as I led everyone to the back of the gym.

We slipped through the window next to the pool and up the steps to the basketball floor. Each team quickly gathered itself to one end of the court to practice and prepare for the war about to happen. I was on Shock's team, and Stump ended up on Riles' team to make it even. A coin was flipped to see who would get the ball first—Riles. The game was on.

It was magical, it was musical, it was entertaining, and it was fun. Not all ten players were as fluid and graceful as Shock and Riles, but they made the others better, even me. I loved to watch these two go at it, and it was what inspired me to play basketball for the next thirty years. From one end of the court to the other, the ball zipped between players, the dribbling was in unison and then a swish, a sound that sent chills up and down anyone's spine that has an appreciation for a ball as it glided through the net.

"Good shot, real good shot there Riles," Shock observed.

Shock always encouraged, even in battle, but this wasn't a battle, no bloodshed, no foul language. In its own special way it was ballet to the other end of the court, where Shock blistered the net from about twenty feet.

"You too, Shock, what a shot," Riles exclaimed.

For the next two hours, there was a constant chorus of compliments from one team to the next. Sneakers up and down the floor, swish here, swish there, constant dribbling of the ball, and it wasn't just a Shock and Riles' show. They made sure their teammates got to participate as well.

What I failed to mention was that there were no referees, no one to call fouls. It was on the honor system, and as a twelve year old kid, I discovered what honor, respect, and appreciation for this opportunity to play ball was about—camaraderie.

There were many, many more times we would sneak, legally or illegally, into the gym to build on these character traits. Sometimes we had to crawl across the beams in order to replace light bulbs. This gym was our cavern of fun. Men like Shock and Riles made growing up in this mill village more entertaining, more exciting, and, yes, more enlightening.

Oh, by the way, who won the game? I don't remember, it really didn't matter.

Chapter 19
W & W Bike Repair

"Who in the world would want us to work on their bikes?" I asked.

Wart and I had decided to go into our own bicycle repair business.

"Our best customer is going to be Zeek," Wart replied. "He's got several friends who might need our help."

"Again, who is going to pay us money to work on his bike? I wouldn't trust either one of us."

"You get the business, and I'll do the work, is that all right?" Wart asked.

We were on our way to inspect Wart's basement to see if it might be a good place to open our bike service, Will and Wart's Bike Repair Shop. Wart's dad was a pretty neat man.

Not neat in the sense of being cool or neat in the sense of being kind and generous, he was neat in how he presented himself and his house. Everything was usually in order and clean. Wart's home was always warm and inviting, and I give most of the credit to his mom, Miss Charlene. She was a strong, Christian housewife and mother who always welcomed Wart's friends with kind words and an occasional snack.

Today, however, we had to inspect Wart's basement, where we would be doing most of the repair work. It had a cement floor and a toolbox filled with tools we could use to fix bicycles. I didn't know anything about tools, but Wart pretended he did. Anyway, everything looked to be in order and promising for our little enterprise.

"My dad has some sawhorses here somewhere," Wart remarked. "We can use them to place the bike on when we're doing repairs."

"Sounds great to me, let's get started," I said. "I'll put the word out that we are in business."

"That's fine with me," Wart replied. "I heard that Zeek was having trouble with his bike, so let's start with him. Make sure he has some money first."

"I will. He'll have to pay up front before we do anything, and then if we have to do extra we can charge him more," I said.

"By the way, how much are we going to charge?" Wart asked.

"Let's start off by charging fifty cents for the normal repairs, and if it calls for something more we can adjust the cost then."

"I hope you boys make a lot of money," Miss Charlene encouraged.

She worked at a clothing store on the square in Gainesville. I believe she really wanted us to do something profitable and beneficial.

I jumped on my bike and took off for Zeek's house, and just happened to run into some kids on the way. I quickly told them about our business, but they seemed uninterested. Like I said, who would want us to work on their bikes?

As I entered Highland Avenue from Carolina Street there was Zeek as he walked his bicycle home, something was wrong, and I sensed an opportunity.

"What's wrong Zeek?" I asked. "Can I give you a hand with your bike?"

"I was on my way home when the front end came loose and almost threw me off," he said.

"Do you think you could fix it for me, Will?"

"Sure, but it's going to cost you some money," I said. "Wart and I just went into the bicycle repair business a few minutes ago. You could be our first customer, and we will give you a discount; how about that?"

"You and Wart went into business? Where? Take me there, I've got some change, and I'll pay you for the repair," he continued.

"Turn around, the repair shop is in Wart's basement," I said.

We turned around, led our bikes back down Carolina, and around to Wart's basement, where he was still getting organized.

"We have our first customer, Wart. It's Zeek, and he needs our help bad. Can you come out and give him an idea of how much it will cost?" I asked.

As Wart was coming out of his basement door, I secretly signaled him that Zeek had fifty cents with him, and he nodded like he knew what I was talking about, without Zeek ever knowing the difference.

"Let's see what we got here," Wart offered, knowing full well what it was going to take to fix his bike. "Zeek, you have to stay outside while Will and I work on your bike. Do you understand?"

"Yeah, no problem Wart, I'll wait right here."

Wart closed the door, and we knew right away, the only repair that bike needed was for us to loosen the nut on the front wheel, slide it back on to the fork and tighten it. We also knew that if we fixed this bike too quickly, Zeek would think he's not getting his money's worth. Fifty cents would be too much to charge, so we went into our stall mode, just enough time to make him think we were serious.

"Grab the handle bars Will and put them in that vise," Wart ordered.

There was no vise, but I knew what Wart was up to.

"Okay, okay, is that good enough for you, Wart?" I asked.

I picked up a small wrench and begin to bang on the sawhorse where Zeek's bike was lying. Wart caught on and grunted and snorted as if he struggled with the tools.

"We are just about done, just a couple of more minutes, and you'll have your bike back," Wart said.

About ten to fifteen minutes passed by before we opened the basement door to give Zeek his bike.

"Try it out, see if it's okay," I said. "Don't go too far in case we have to come get you."

He started up Carolina Street faster than I have ever seen him pedal before and was back down at the shop in no time.

"This bike is better than the day I got it brand new. Boy, you guys are good," he exclaimed.

"That will be fifty cents. We told you we would give you a discount. Now go tell others about our business; we need the money," I said.

As Zeek left on his newly reconditioned, suped-up bike, Wart and I laughed. Immediately, we walked across the street to Miss Irene's cloth shop. She also sold peanuts and ice cold soft drinks. Growing up in the village, one of the treats we seldom got to enjoy was a soft drink with peanuts. We would pour the small bag of nuts into the drink bottle and have our refreshment.

We had no sooner finished the drink and nuts when Zeek's neighbor, Burney, came to see us. He was having bicycle problems, too.

Burney was another MilliKid who lived in the neighborhood. He was several years younger than most of us, but he was a good kid. He never caused trouble and just wanted to be one of us. He laughed a lot, seemed like he always had a good time. He had this blue shaded bike, not sure of the brand, but his rear wheel was crooked. Wart and I knew this job was too much for us.

"Burney, I'm sorry, but we can't help you with this problem. Looks like you might need a new wheel," I said.

He was disappointed and had a sad look on his face. We weren't prepared for this. Wart had an extra bicycle wheel in the back room of his basement. Wart offered this wheel to Burney if it would fit, and it did.

We put Burney's bike on the sawhorses and removed the damaged wheel. When it was off, we slipped Wart's old wheel on and it fit beautifully. Burney was thrilled.

"Thanks, guys. My bike had fallen out of the back of my uncle's truck, and he didn't offer to pay for it. How much do I owe you?" he asked.

"You don't owe me anything; the wheel is Wart's, ask him," I said.

"How much for the wheel, Wart?" Burney asked.

Wart came over to me and asked me privately what I thought. The wheel wasn't mine, we were in Wart's basement, and we used Wart's dad's tools. I really had no say in this discussion, but I had an idea. I shared it with Wart, and he agreed.

"Burney, we might need the parts from your old wheel to fix other kid's bicycles, so let us keep the old wheel, and you just buy Will and me a drink and a pack of peanuts from Miss Irene's. Is that fair?" asked Wart.

"Absolutely! That sounds like a great deal to me. Come on Zeek," Burney urged, "and I'll buy yours, too. If it weren't for you, my bike wouldn't have been fixed."

Everybody was happy. A cold RC with a bag of nuts floating in the top made for a perfect day. Wart's dad wasn't too happy that we used his tools in his basement, so our little endeavor didn't last long.

Chapter 20
Bible School Blues

Bible School always seemed to interfere with my plans during the first week of summer. For one week, I had to wait until almost dinner time before my friends were ready to play. All my friends had to go to Bible School. I have never understood the purpose of Bible School. Even today, fifty years later, it appears to me that the main purpose bible school served was to give the parents an extra week away from their children during the morning. Another purpose was probably to make the volunteers who taught Bible School feel more purposeful, useful, and in touch with God. Nevertheless, it interfered with my plans.

Little Dink, Stump, Wart, Rusty, the Daniels kids, and most of the other neighborhood brats usually attended. I would wait patiently on my front porch for them to get out. Funny, I never saw any heart changes in my friends after it ended. They were the typical bratty kids regardless. By the time we finally got together, we had all sorts of meanness, I mean events, planned. Truthfully, I felt like I was being left out or behind in this case. I was jealous, but they never knew it.

"It's about time you guys got out, what did you do today?" I asked.

"Nothing much as usual," Little Dink was quick to respond, "Except for this sucker in my mouth. I mainly go for the snacks anyway."

"How about you, Wart? Did you learn anything today?" I asked.

"No, I went to get Mama off my back," Wart said, and then he continued to mock his mother, "Wart, honey, you gotta go to Bible school, Lord knows you need it," he said in a whiny voice, "You been a bad boy this week, now go on, and maybe you'll learn something."

Stump piped in, "I had to go because Mama teaches Bible School, and she doesn't trust me out here when she's over there. I ain't learned nothing. I'm ready to have fun. What you got planned, Will?"

"Don't believe anything Little Dink tells you. He gets behind a curtain and takes a nap anyway. The only reason he goes is to get something free to eat and drink," Rusty said.

"We've got a baseball game today with the Daniels' boys and their cousin. We need two more guys, so Zeek and Burney have agreed to play," I said. "Go home, change, bring your gloves and we'll meet in the Daniels' backyard at one."

It wasn't hot yet, early June, but it sure was sunny and muggy. There were about eight of us all together when we assembled at one o'clock. There were Jules, his brother Gibson, their cousin, Smedley, and we let them have Burney, to make things even. We had played a couple of innings, and they drilled us. It was time to take a dinner break, none of us had eaten. Everybody scattered and agreed to meet back as soon as dinner was over. Mama had hotdogs, which was always a summer treat, so Little Dink stopped at my house to eat.

"We need a plan to beat those boys," Little Dink said. "They're really good today. That dang Wart keeps striking out, leaving men on base, and they're killing us."

"I'll talk to Jules and Gibson, maybe they'll let me take his last strike if we agree to let them take Burney's." I said.

Burney passed by our house on his way back to the field.

"Hey Burney, come here a second. I need to talk to you, boy," I said with some authority.

"We're getting whipped down there. I tell you what, they are going to ask to take your last strike. Agree to it, but make sure you hit the ball so they won't have to," I pleaded. "I promise if you do what I ask, you will be on my team next time, okay?"

"Why would I want to be on your team next time? We're trashing you guys. I don't like anybody taking my last strike anyway," he answered.

"All right, if that's the case, you won't be included tonight when we play fox-and-hounds in the gym," I threatened.

"That's not fair. You always let me play with you guys in the gym," he said.

"Not tonight, not if we don't have a deal."

He paused for a moment, looked me in the eyes, started to giggle and said, "You really do want to beat them bad, don't you?"

"Do we have a deal or not?"

"Yeah, no problem."

The teams gathered back after dinner in the Daniel's backyard. It was our turn at bat.

"What if we take Wart's third strike, and you guys take Burney's? Is that acceptable?" I asked.

"Why not? You're so far behind now it doesn't matter anyway," Jules said.

"You're not taking my last strike Will, no way, not today. I'm playing too good," Wart said.

"Playing good, you haven't been on base yet, you dimwit," Little Dink declared. "Will's taking your last strike, and that's that."

"He won't get a chance to. I'll hit the ball before the third pitch."

Sure enough, Little Dink was on second base with Stump on first and two outs with Wart up to bat.

Bible School Blues

"Jules, slow it down and throw me one about right here," he held out his bat indicating where he wanted the pitch.

Jules tried his best to get Wart to hit the ball.

"Strike one!" Little Dink announced from second base.

Wart wasn't too happy about missing an easy one, so he begged Jules again to throw it to a certain area.

"Strike two!" Little Dink declared.

"Okay, step aside, Wart, but remember to run the bases when I hit the ball," I said.

Wart took his position off to my right side since I was a left-handed batter and positioned himself to run. He wasn't too happy about it either.

"Come on Jules, throw it in here, boy. You might not find this one," I bragged.

Jules tossed it nice and easy right where I liked it best. I gripped the bat even tighter and swung with every ounce of strength I had in me...

Fwaaappp, Kathunk, Uhh.

What began as one of the most beautiful sounds in this world quickly became one of the worst noises I have ever heard.

I made terrific contact with the ball and even better contact with Wart's chest. He stood too close. Down he went. I forgot about the ball. I fell to my knees to check on Wart. He couldn't catch his breath, he turned purple and for a moment I thought he was going to die.

"Will, help me, Will, help me, I can't breathe," Wart forced out of his airless lungs.

I had heard about and even seen mouth-to-mouth resuscitation, but I didn't want to put my mouth on Wart's. He lay there, almost lifeless, so I grabbed his belt like I had watched on TV and picked him up just off the ground, moved his knees into a kneeling position.

"Wart, talk to me, boy, can you breathe yet? I am so sorry, I didn't mean to hit you," I said softly.

Everyone was quiet and scared. Wart was small, which made this even more severe, but he started to get his color back and finally he sat up.

"Somebody, go get his mama," I begged.

"No, no, no, don't get her. She'll call an ambulance and freak out," Wart said. "Just give me a couple of minutes to get to my feet."

I kept apologizing, and swore I would never take his last strike again, which turned out to be a lie. I had him stand in a different place from then on. Wart stood and decided he had enough excitement for one day and went to sit under a shady tree to recuperate. One of the Daniels' kids went inside their house to get Wart some water and a cold towel.

We didn't play baseball again for a few days, and when we did we took extra caution to make sure that sort of mishap wouldn't happen again. We had other accidents but nothing quite that serious. Wart was out of commission for a while. His mother never knew it, but he had an incredible bruise on his chest for some time.

By the way, we never found the ball. All of us lost interest in that game anyway, and it didn't matter who won. What did matter was that Wart was okay, and he lived to play another day. I never gave him or the rest of my friends a hard time about Bible School again.

Chapter 21
Joyful Noise Janitor

"Boys, be quiet, church service is in progress. We can't hear the preacher because of you guys!" Miss Emo exclaimed as she stepped out on the church porch. "You need to go somewhere else; try the ball field," she said, "or just somewhere, but go!"

My, how things had changed. It wasn't that long ago, before the previous pastor left, that we voluntarily moved to someone's backyard or the gym because the church was so *loud*. With all the songs and music, we weren't able to play in our normal spots during Sunday evening church services. Even the preacher during those years could be heard throughout the neighborhood.

We were on Quarry Street one evening when he was high on the pulpit. You could actually hear him three blocks away.

We used to think maybe he thought he could disrupt the service at the Baptist church, which was on Quarry. Anyway, people used to park up and down both sides of Spring Street, around Myrtle Drive and on Highland Avenue—this place bustled with excitement. These days, however, they were fortunate to have ten people attend. We could barely hear them singing, and we never knew when the preacher started.

"Okay guys, you heard her, let's move. How about your backyard Wart?" I asked.

"Not mine. Daddy's not in a good mood and Mama's not there. She's at the other church," he said.

The *other* denomination was New Holland Baptist, where most of us were either members or pretended to belong. Around the turn of the twentieth century, the Methodist church was built to serve both Methodists and Baptists, until the Baptists built their own church in 1951. Generally, they would rotate Sundays and sometimes one denomination would attend in the morning while the other attended at night. Two separate congregations and even two pastors, but it worked for a while until *the incident* occurred.

It was in the late 50s, I can't be sure exactly when, but the ghost in the auditorium was being seen more and more, especially at night. I was just seven or eight, but knew better than to go near that spooky cavern. The auditorium was built after the church around 1921, and was used for plays and to show an occasional movie for the community.

Legend has it, that a man named Parks Greer was the custodian for the church and auditorium. I can't say I ever met

Joyful Noise Janitor

him, but I believe to this day that I have seen his ghostly shadow on more than one occasion. It terrified many of us kids and led to the auditorium being condemned and eventually dismantled, brick by brick, in 1960.

Shortly before the Baptist church was built, the Methodist church decided to celebrate its twenty-fifth anniversary. It was an overcast but warm spring day on a Sunday afternoon. Parks had been busy for several days getting the church and auditorium ready and, according to some of his friends, was very proud of the job he had done. Members began filing in and filling up the church, the auditorium, and the surrounding grounds. People from everywhere were in attendance. They wanted to join in on the fun and celebrate this historic moment. Not all the people in the village went to this church, but they wanted to join the celebration. Food and beverage were abundant. Everyone seemed happy.

"Will, do you still believe that the auditorium was haunted?" Little Dink asked. "Daddy says he knew Mr. Greer and after the events that occurred during the twenty-fifith anniversary of the auditorium, things were never the same around here. What have you heard, Will?"

"Wait a second, just wait a second, will you?" Stump chimed in. "What do you mean the auditorium was haunted? I have never heard this story."

"Your folks are new to New Holland, Stump," I said. "Go on home and ask your mom or dad if they have ever heard of the *Joyful Noise Janitor*."

"All right, I'll be right back. Can somebody walk with me to the street light?" Stump asked with a nervous tone in his voice.

"What's the matter, Stump, you scared already?" I asked laughingly, hiding my own discomfort.

In a way, I was sort of glad it was him that had the long walk home. I was starting to get the jitters myself, and I was only twenty feet from the front of my house.

"Never mind, I don't need any company. I'll be back here in a few minutes."

We hadn't noticed, but with all the talk about the church, the auditorium, and Mr. Greer, twilight time was upon us. We waited and waited for Stump to return, but he didn't and we decided to go home and revisit this conversation tomorrow.

"Hey, Will, you up?" Little Dink asked the next morning.

"Yeah, give me a minute," I said as I looked out my upstairs bedroom window.

"Have you seen Stump?" I asked. "He was probably so scared he couldn't get any sleep."

"Stump and his dad are over there talking, standing where the auditorium once stood."

The only thing left from the auditorium was the foundation. We walked over to where they were and could tell Stump's dad was not amused with us. He adjusted his glasses and asked…

"Why are you guys making up stories and scaring my son? Stump couldn't sleep last night and insisted that there is some sort of ghost story associated with the auditorium. Is that right?" he asked.

"That's what we've heard," I said nervously.

"Heard from whom?"

"Just heard,"

"I'll go ask Ole Lady Stover. She's been around here forever, she'll know," he said.

It wasn't three minutes or so that Stump's dad and Ole Lady Stover came walking back to where the auditorium once stood. Stump's dad turned and walked home. The MilliKids were all scared of her. She was never married and was always gruff and mean to us. But we were curious to hear what she had to say.

"So, you boys have heard of Parks Greer, the janitor?" she asked.

She smiled. We had never seen her smile, but it was a wickedly sly smile, the kind one gets when he or she knows something strange and is not comfortable sharing the information with others.

"Parks was one of the kindest men I have ever met or known," she began. "Yes, he was the janitor in the church and auditorium, and he was known for the cleanliness of those two buildings. He sang while he worked. What a beautiful voice! Back in the late 40s, we were celebrating the church's anniversary and people from all over came. It didn't matter if they were Methodists or not. They felt a connection to this community and joined in on the fun that day. There were songs, music, kids playing, and plenty of food. Not only that, it was the end of World War II, and soldiers were returning from war, so this was kind of a welcome home party for them as well."

"But, Miss Stover," Little Dink started, "how did you know Parks Greer?"

"Just hold on, son, I'll get to that in a moment."

"The neighborhood kids had put on a short play in the auditorium, and Parks had started to clean as soon as they finished. He was in a hurry, he had plans, and he knew he had to start his cleanup early. He was on the stage singing and cleaning and began to draw the curtain, a huge curtain with long ties, or ropes as some would later call them. Anyway, he had to scale up a ladder to fix a snag in one of the curtains. Somehow, one of the ropes twisted around him and prevented him from freeing it. He called for help, and one of the men of the church, Mr. Miller, was steadying the ladder when Parks fell. Before Mr. Miller could help him, Parks had fallen at least twenty feet onto the hardwood floors of the auditorium. He was rushed immediately to the hospital, where he died."

"He died?" Wart uttered.

"That's sad," Little Dink said.

"Why was he in such a hurry? What were his big plans?" I asked.

"As part of the celebration and because one of Park's brothers was returning from being overseas during the war," a long pause…"Parks and I were getting married that afternoon."

Silence. Not one word for moments.

"It's okay, boys. Until they tore the auditorium down in 1960, I thought I could see his shadow in that upper room straight across from my bedroom," as she pointed to her house and her bedroom.

"He comforted me for years until they dismantled the auditorium."

It had to be the same shadow I saw on several occasions. I guess Ole Lady Stover had a right to be angry. But since she shared that story with us, she seemed to smile more often and wave to us from time to time. Maybe she just needed to share her misery with others. Maybe, just maybe, Stump's dad knew we needed to hear it.

Chapter 22

Carolina Crash

"We don't need anybody else. We have enough, three on one team and four on the other. That's plenty," I insisted. "My team will only have three players; that's all I need to win."

"Zeek will play. I'll go get him," Wart said. "Let me get my bike, and I'll see if he wants to join us, but he's not going to be on my team. He will be on your team, Will. You are not taking my last strike today."

The MilliKids had planned this Saturday morning in early June. They knew Rusty would be at his Granny's, so a day of baseball at the New Holland ball field was in the works. Most of the time, we wouldn't even make it to the ball field. We would just settle in someone's backyard and play there. As usual, whoever had Wart on his team had the option of taking his last strike. That is, if Wart had two strikes on him, then whoever was the leader of his team could take his last swing at the ball, hopefully to avoid an out. It was around ten o'clock in the morning, not quite hot yet, and the crew was ready to play ball. Only one problem, we were a player short.

Zeek was one of the crew at times, when we needed someone. Later on, he became an almost full-time member. He was several years younger, but we could count on him in a pinch. Today, we needed him. Zeek would do most anything the other kids told him to do, which is why he was often invited to participate. He was always grateful to be included. He too was like a little brother most of us didn't have.

The teams had already been stacked…I mean decided, with my team hopefully having the edge. Heck, we all wanted to win and were quick to point out any lopsidedness on the teams if it appeared that way. Anyway, we had all gathered in Rusty's grandmother's side yard waiting for the teams to be assembled before we hustled down to the ball park or the nearest inviting backyard.

That day, it was me, Little Dink, Stump, Wart, Rusty, and two other kids in the village who were really not MilliKids, but we let them play sometimes just to even things out. All we needed now was one more player. Wart went to get his bike to pick up Zeek.

Wart always showed off on his bicycle, and this morning was no different. He pretended his bike had a motor and he would provide the sound. He was comical at times, even pretended to change gears. Looking back, it seemed kind of strange—it was, and so was Wart. Anyway, he provided all the sound effects needed to make it sound like his bike had an engine.

"*Vrudden, vrudden, vrudden,*" snorted Wart as he climbed Carolina Street, which was pretty close to being about a thirty degree uphill grade. With all that noise he made, one would expect him to get to the top quicker.

As Wart popped a wheelie to show off, the chain separated from the sprocket, but Wart was able to control the bike. He flipped it over and quickly proceeded to re-engage the chain. Something every kid should know how to do. He flipped it back right side up, and off he went, with additional sputters and groans for our benefit. We could hear him when he was out of sight. We were all bent over in laughter.

By this time, we sat on the grassy bank in Rusty's Granny's yard just talking, waiting on Wart and Zeek to get back. We could hear them on their way. Kids did not realize how their voices echoed through the village, which made us laugh even more as we heard them while they hustled back.

They came around Spring Street and onto Highland Avenue, destined for Carolina to make our teams complete. Our laughter became more intense when we saw Wart and his passenger, Zeek, as he sat on the front handlebars, legs spread to each side of the front wheel. We could barely see Wart's face behind Zeek. They turned onto Carolina with thoughts of cruising to a stop on Granny's grassy bank next to all of us. As Wart attempted to slow and jump the curb to where we were, we heard this distinctive *snap*, followed by an ear-piercing grinding. Then came *zeel, zeel* sounds that we had never heard, but we knew why. The chain had popped off again and Wart could not stop it this time. Down Carolina they went, both of them screaming and shouting for help.

"Somebody help! Please God help us," Wart yelled. Zeek cried and looked up to the heavens for a miracle.

There was nothing we could do. Stump and I started to run down Carolina to help, but soon realized we couldn't catch them. We all laughed in fear, but somehow still enjoyed the moment that eventually became a memory none of us would ever forget.

Wart was able to steer across Mr. Collins' driveway and into his own yard where his dad's pickup truck was parked. He, Zeek, and the bike disappeared briefly as they flipped over the bank that separated the Collins' yard from Wart's. All we could see was the side of Wart's dad's truck, a sky blue Chevy, which was about to be used for a backstop. The bike flipped rear-end over front-end, with two flailing bodies and butts straight up in the air.

Karoomp, kahoom. The bike and two MilliKids were now embedded in the side of a pickup truck. Laughter ended for a moment. This had become very serious. Would insurance pay for this kind of damage to a truck?

"Oh, ohh, geesh, what in the world happened?" Wart moaned.

"Oh, my head. Oh, my head. Oh, my God, Pearl's gonna kill me," Zeek cried.

"What have you boys done now," yelled Wart's dad as he ran out of the house when he heard all the commotion. "My truck better not be damaged, or both of you'll get even more. Get in the house, boy. I'll be right in there to take care of you in just a minute," he continued, and "the rest of you boys get out of here right now."

We helped Zeek to his feet and fled. No baseball today. As we settled back on Granny's bank, a big knot had surfaced on Zeek's head, and I knew I had to get him home.

"I'll take him. Pearl's not going to believe him, but maybe she'll believe me." I said.

Pearl was Zeek's grandmother, who lived with them and took care of Zeek and his brother and sisters while their mom was at work. I carried him home in my arms. We were about halfway there when Zeek said he could walk. I put him down, and we continued to his house. Pearl sat on the front porch in a swing. She noticed us several hundred feet away. She had to be 110 years old then, but here she came. She took care of those children and was serious about it.

Nobody messed with Pearl's grandkids.

"What have you done now?" she asked Zeek. "Go on home, Will. I'll talk to your mama later."

"Talk to *my* mama," I muttered to myself. I wasn't sure what that meant, but figured that by the time she talked to my mama Zeek would have set her straight on what happened, instead of me getting the blame. I got blamed for just about everything that went wrong in the village. It didn't matter—Will did it. It wasn't two hours later that Zeek and Little Dink were at my house, and we all had a good laugh about the whole ordeal. Zeek had a big knot on his forehead—thank goodness he had a hard head. That's one of the reasons he was invited to join us. We knew he would attempt things we wouldn't dare think of doing. His head was just that hard.

Wart didn't come around for several days. I'm not sure why, and I don't remember asking him about what his dad did to him (if he did anything at all) but it really didn't matter. Wart was back to normal before long, or I say should abnormal. Nothing was normal to us.

Now that I think about it, that day was probably Zeek's initiation into becoming a MilliKid. Even though he wasn't always included, (too young for some of our other antics) he did earn his stripes. He survived! He laughed about it for years. You have to laugh at yourself if you want to be a true MilliKid. We had many reasons to cry, but we had far more reasons to laugh.

Chapter 23
Suislide on Spring

Snow? On occasion, maybe an inch or two. If we were lucky, there would be some ice, sleet, freezing rain, and if we were really fortunate, school was canceled. In any event, it seldom snowed in the village, but when it did come it was truly majestic, beautiful, and uncorrupted by pollution. It was an awesome sight, and it caused everyone to get excited, especially us MilliKids.

"Right between your eyes, Wart. Here it comes and you better run, boy," I urged.

Wart was a nuisance on this day and we would like nothing better than to send him home in tears with a big knot between his eyes. Little Dink and I had just about enough of his antics so we gave chase. Wart could run, but he couldn't outrun us. As he crossed the ditch that separated his backyard from Miss Icie's, we nailed him and nailed him good. Little Dink and I unleashed a flurry of snowballs on his backside and you could hear the *thump, kathump* as the snowballs found their target.

"Oh, Yeow, that's enough, I'm telling Mama on you," he exclaimed as he crawled back to his house.

Little Dink and I fell over in laughter and then got pelted. It seemed Wart had some friends after all. We hadn't noticed, but Stump, Zeek, and Rusty were on our tails and decided to retaliate a little for Wart. Little Dink and I took refuge behind an old oak tree in Wart's backyard and to collect our arsenal of snowballs, or rather iceballs, when the fun really began.

"Bring it on, boys," Little Dink taunted. "Better go get your mamas and when you do they better come prepared."

The barrage was on, snowball after snowball flew through the air, seldom hitting its target.

"You got a weenie for an arm, Stump," I said. "Maybe your mama will teach you how to throw better," I kept on...*Fwaapppp*, "Oh, my ear, my ear."

That one hurt, and it made me mad. Stump and Zeek laughed so hard they didn't notice when I started toward them. As they turned to escape, I tackled them both and we sprawled down the hill, almost to Papa Dan's yard. We all laughed, no serious injuries, just a few scrapes and scratches from the ice when it made contact with our skin.

"Did you hear that more snow is predicted tonight?" Zeek asked.

"Daddy said that school has already been canceled for tomorrow," Stump said.

"Are you kidding me, no way," Little Dink said.

"Yep, I heard it, too," Zeek said.

We had just brushed the snow off our clothes when Wart's mom shouted to us, "Boys, you behave and leave Wart alone. Can he come over and play now? I promise he'll behave."

Wart's mom was standing outside near the porch making his case for him.

"Sure, Miss Charlene, he'll be okay with us," I said.

Stump was ready to turn one loose when he caught my attention, and I warned him otherwise.

"Not her, Stump. She's a kind old lady, not that you could hit her from here anyway."

MilliKids didn't stay mad long. They couldn't. They had no one else to play with and besides, we were all just one big, mostly happy family. Wart sloshed back over like nothing had happened, everything almost normal again.

"You know what we haven't done in a long time?" I asked. "Sledding, I mean sliding. Who's got some cardboard?"

None of us could afford a sled. There was really no need for one, as seldom as it snowed.

"Mama and Daddy just bought a new stove from Chamber's Hardware," Little Dink said. "I bet the cardboard box is still under the house in the basement."

"I'm hungry. It's time for lunch," Stump said. "Let's get together in an hour and do some sliding."

We all went home for lunch, Wart came with me. We thawed out and then had something to eat. Usually, Mama had on a pot of beans, creamed potatoes, cornbread, and slaw, and there was always enough to go around. Wart was welcome, and he knew it. We had eaten at each other's house from time to time.

"You know, Wart, if we can get that cardboard from Little Dink's and maybe one more person, we might just have a race," I said with a shiver.

"As much ice and sleet as there is, sliding ought to be fast and fun," he said. "Why don't we go down Spring Street today instead of the terraces?"

"I don't know, we can't take much of a chance. Never know how bad traffic is at the bottom of the hill."

"We'll have a spotter down there to look out for traffic and warn us just in case," Wart said.

"We'll see. Let's eat," I said.

We had no sooner eaten, when Little Dink showed up with the piece of cardboard from his place and across Spring Street came Stump with a huge piece that he had found.

"This is going to be fun," I said.

Suislide on Spring

We suited back up, went out front to the top of Spring Street and stood there as we looked toward the bottom of the hill.

"Who's first?" I asked.

"You are, Will. You don't ever go first. It's time for you to show us the way," Stump said.

"No, that wouldn't be fair. It was Wart's idea to slide down Spring so let's let him go first," I said. "But, we will need someone at the bottom of the hill to watch out for oncoming cars."

I knew I didn't want to go first. That's what we had Wart for—just in case something went terribly wrong.

"That will be me," volunteered Stump. "Now watch for my signal. If my hands are out straight like this," he demonstrated a safe sign, like in baseball, "that means it's okay to come on down, but if I hold my hands up like this," again he demonstrated by holding both hands up in front of him with the palms facing the slider, "that means stop."

Spring Street is at least 300 feet long and steep, so whoever was on the cardboard was going to be really fast by the time he reached the bottom of the hill. We had never slid on the street before, so this was new territory for all of us.

Wart took the piece of cardboard and bent the front part of it up about twelve to fifteen inches so he could get a good hold on it. He braced himself behind the bent piece. He folded his legs and gave Stump the signal that he was ready. Stump looked both ways, then he motioned for Wart to come. We shoved Wart and the cardboard for about ten feet, and then he took off. He was flying before he got halfway down the hill. We started to laugh and carried on a little and then noticed Stump suddenly held his hands up trying to get Wart to stop.

"Stop! Stop! Wart, stop!" Stump yelled.

It was too late, and I don't believe Wart heard him anyway. You could see Wart's butt bouncing up and down on the cardboard as it flew. We stood in amazement and awe. I don't believe any of us thought to pray at that moment; it was probably too late for God, too.

Stump attempted to run up the hill to try and stop Wart, but he slipped and fell awkwardly to the side.

Swoosh, phtt, phtt went Wart.

We were about to lose a MilliKid, and there was nothing we could do. Stump had put both his hands on top of his head and ducked so he wouldn't have to look.

Swoosh, splat, kasplat went Wart as he darted between and avoided two cars coming in opposite directions. It was miraculous. It was legendary. It was Wart. He survived the inevitable that awaited him. There was no collision. He sailed across Highway 23 and crashed into the fence next to the mill without one scratch. Amazing, somehow he made it. We all cheered and ran to congratulate Wart. He was mad. He thought Stump had given him the wrong signal on purpose.

When we got to Wart, he didn't know whether to laugh or cry. You could tell he was scared, but he didn't want us to notice. We helped him up, gave a couple of pats on the back and brushed the snow and ice off.

That was the end of our little adventure on Spring Street for the day. We quickly retreated to the terraces in our backyards and enjoyed the snow and ice while it lasted. School was canceled the next day, but the snow and ice had almost melted, making it hard to slide. Anyway, we had our fun, thanks to Wart. He was hard to deal with for awhile, but he had earned it.

Chapter 24
MilliKat

Jacob was an ordinary, good-for-nothing tomcat who loved to stay by my side regardless of what I was doing or how the weather was. He was always around. I don't remember Little Dink, Stump, or Wart having any pets, but they all loved Jacob. He was funny. I wasn't much of a cat lover growing up, but Jacob changed that. He ate what we ate, and he went where we went. This day was no different; it was a rainy, cool fall day. Just cool enough to wear a light jacket. Jacob and I were outside wondering what to do next. He carefully examined my every move.

Stump was on his way over to my house. I had made sure he was aware my plans that day really didn't include him, but he decided to come anyway. None of us MilliKids liked to stay in the house if there was any possibility of going outside.

"I hate the fall," Stump blasted as he skipped across Spring Street.

I could tell he was going to be lots of fun today.

"I have an idea," I said. "We're going to have a pop-up contest with my ball and old wooden bat."

Stump wasn't very good, and I figured if I embarrassed him enough he would just go home. I wanted to be alone for some reason anyway.

"Okay Stump, here's the deal," I said. "We're going to see who can hit the ball the farthest and the most accurate from my side yard to Mr. Collins' side yard, and you're going first."

The Collins lived directly behind us, and our backyards butted each other.

"Give me the ball and bat and watch out, it's about time somebody put you in your place," he challenged. "You think you're better than the rest of us; well, let's see."

I always liked a challenge, especially if I knew for sure the other person didn't have a chance—and Stump didn't. He wasn't bad, he wasn't pitiful, just overconfident, and I had him where I wanted him. They call it "trash talk" today, but back then we knew how to get under each other's skin—and he was doing a pretty good job of getting under mine.

"Let's see it, big boy," I said.

"Yeah, yeah, yeah, I know, I know, we play by your rules when we are in your yard. By the way, it seems we play by your rules when we are in somebody else's yard, including mine," he barked. "But get out of the way, and let me show you how it's done."

About that time, Little Dink arrived and started barking his own brand of harassment at both of us. Stump tossed the ball in the air, and, whiff, he missed. Little Dink and I started to cackle and poke more fun at him.

"It's the rain, the bat's slippery, I get another chance," Stump snapped back.

He placed the bat between his legs to dry it off.

"Come on, Stump, watch out now, the rain might get in your eyes," Little Dink said aggravatingly.

Stump tossed the ball again, and he made full contact this time. It went all of twenty feet. Immediately, Little Dink and I doubled over in laughter. There's one thing that really got to Stump, and that's when he was being made fun of, he was not nice to be around. By the way, all of us MilliKids liked to show off, especially in front of each other.

"You better go see if you can find the ball," Little Dink urged. "Oh yeah, there it is, you're about to step on it."

Little Dink and I burst out in laughter again. The day was beginning to shape up after all.

"Give me the bat and ball, Stump, and stand back," I ordered. "Take notes on how it's done right."

I tossed the ball and "thump," up, up, and away, higher and higher, the ball just about went out of sight. It landed squarely in Mr. Collins' side yard, almost perfect.

I jogged over to where the ball had landed, and quickly tossed it up and hit back to where Stump stood. I pretended like I did this all the time, and in a way I did. When I returned to my side yard, both Stump and Little Dink issued a challenge for me to do it again.

"Just a minute, hold on," Little Dink urged. "If you are so good why don't you put it on Wart's roof? I don't believe you can hit it that far."

"If I hit it on Wart's roof, you'll have to go get it."

Wart lived next door to the Collins', and it was a good poke to hit one that distance, but I really felt like I could do it.

All along, Jacob, my cat, sat harmlessly to the side. He escorted me to and from Mr. Collins' yard. He sat by himself on the side as he waited for me to hit another one. The mist had gotten heavier, and the fog was thick, but I had been challenged, and I would not back down. Jacob was covered with mist, and his fur was all fluffed up, I guess because he had his own fun as he rolled around in the grass.

I could tell the bat was more slippery than usual, but I tried to dry it off by sliding it back and forth between my pant legs.

Actually, my intention was to hit the ball over Wart's house. I had done this before but never under these conditions.

"Hurry it up, Will, are you going to do it or not?" Stump said.

I tossed the ball straight up, and I tried to find all the strength within me to shut these two up. As the ball descended, and it seemed like slow motion, I put my entire body into the swing. *Kawhump* went the ball, and *shuh, shuh, shuh* went the bat with a helicopter type motion and sound. It slipped out of my hands. The bat headed toward Jacob. He didn't see it, and I couldn't react quick enough to save him. *Fwap* into the side of Jacob's head. He flipped over about three times and lay completely still. Before anyone could say anything, Little Dink and Stump were gone (and I mean in a flash) in the direction of their homes. They wanted nothing to do with this, and I didn't blame them — this was all on me.

I started to cry. Jacob lay there, no sound, no movement. I knew I had killed my buddy as I tried to show off for my friends. I rolled him over. His eyes were shut, and his mouth was open with his tongue hanging out. I thought he was dead. How was I going to tell Mama, what was I going to do? I had heard about mouth-to-mouth resuscitation even at this early age, but I had never attempted it, especially on a wet, shriveled-up cat.

Tears flooded my face, and I honestly felt like running too, but I was already home and nowhere to run. I reached down to lift Jacob to take him inside. Why, I don't know, suddenly, it was important to dry him off. As I lifted him I could feel movement. I placed him back on the ground as he started to breathe again. I helped him to his feet, and he stood upright. I believe I thanked God right then and there for saving my cat.

My tears turned to relief, and as I stroked him he looked up at me. He shook his head over and over, he looked at me again. I looked straight into his eyes, one of them was crossed — I mean out-of-whack. One eye appeared perfect, but his right eye was off somewhat. It kind of stared off on its own to the left. I shook his head as I tried to straighten it, but it didn't work. Jacob tried to walk, but he walked around in circles. I picked him up, took him to my room because I wasn't quite ready to tell Mama what had happened. I put him on the floor, and again he walked around in circles. He did this for several days until he learned how to balance himself to walk straight again.

Jacob was not the same from that day on. He did learn how to walk, but he was different. He stayed by my side even more. I couldn't go anywhere without him. After what I had done he loved me even more. I guess, in a weird sort of way, he knew I didn't mean him any harm and would never do anything to hurt him. He and I were buddies until he disappeared two years later, and I don't believe it was because he couldn't find his way back home.

Chapter 25
Witch Hazel

The MilliKids had the pasture to play in and we occasionally made up games and stories to go along with it. We spent many days in the pasture, or "woods" as we casually called it. Years earlier our local residents raised their livestock there, which helped put food and money on the table. By the time our set of MilliKids came along, no one raised livestock or had any interest in the woods except us.

It was another one of the havens we often roamed in, and where we learned to shoot our BB guns. Sometimes, our days were spent there and many fond memories were rooted in those woods, which served as another playground for us. There were several pigsties that remained, and we often found ourselves huddled up in one when it rained. The sty was actually a small wooden shed.

Little Dink, Stump, and I had decided that we were going to turn one of these little sheds into a cabin. It needed a lot of work, but we were able to gather planks, nails, hammers, and whatever else we needed to make it more comfortable. We had spent three days working on it when Stump decided to create our own witch story to make the shed more personal and private. We didn't want any other kids to play in it or claim it, so "Witch Hazel" was created from own little devilish minds, and it served us well for a while…until Witch Hazel decided to come to life.

"Man, I'm tired. I think we have done just about enough, what do you think?" Little Dink asked.

"Yeah, it's time we have some fun with this place before it falls in," I replied.

"You know, we did a pretty good job getting it fixed up and all. Not that I would want to spend the night in it, if you know what I mean," Stump added.

"As soon as Wart and Rusty find out about it, this place will really be crowded," I said.

"They don't need to know. They haven't helped in any way, and besides, they wouldn't know how to take care of it," Little Dink offered.

"It's time to have some fun with Zeek. We'll convince him that a witch lives here and wants to see him," I said.

Ordinarily, we didn't try to scare the neighborhood kids unless we had an ulterior motive, usually to keep them away from whatever it was we were working on. But today was different. We wanted to put a little scare in Zeek. He was still very young and impressionable, and I believed we could pull it off.

We took a short cut through the woods to the rear of Zeek's house. We didn't notice anyone at first, but when we came closer to his side porch we could hear people as they talked, and we knew he was there. This was our opportunity. Little Dink, Stump, and I began to run and yell to get their attention. We pretended to be frightened and told the story about the discovery of Witch Hazel. Zeek was immediately scared and turned to go into his house.

"Wait a minute, Zeek, you have to help us," Little Dink urged. "We just discovered a witch living in a little shack in the woods, and she wants to talk with you."

"What do you mean talk to me? I'm not talking to no witch," he blurted. "No sir, you won't get me to go talk to no witch."

"Zeek, she caught us as we looked into her shack, and before we knew it she had us surrounded with broomsticks," I said.

"I've got you boys now, and if you don't bring me that little Fowler kid I will visit all three of you tonight at bedtime," the witch declared.

"She was serious Zeek. If you don't go talk to her we'll be in trouble," Stump insisted.

We sat there on Zeek's front porch for a few minutes. He said he would go if we went with him for protection. It was as if he really didn't believe us at first, but there was also a little curiosity on his part.

"You guys are going to have to wait 'til after supper," Stump said. "I'm hungry and I'm not going anywhere until I eat."

Stump pretended like he was going home for supper. He did go home, got an old dress and apron that belonged to his mom, and found a scarf to go on his head. We had prearranged this to give him enough time to get back to the shack in the woods, change and wait there for Zeek and us.

It wasn't but just a few minutes when I noticed Stump as he sneaked behind the Hick's house on his way to the shack.

"Let's go, Zeek," I said, "Stump won't come back, and Witch Hazel waits for you."

Little Dink, Zeek, and I started for the shack. It was near twilight, and the sun was almost gone, quite eerie like, but we went anyway. We were about halfway down the bank before we crossed the creek, and here came Stump…as he screamed and yelled at the top of his lungs.

"There really is a witch over there," Stump loudly warned, "and she's after me."

I thought he had changed our plans, and it seemed like a good idea at first, but when we looked up to the top of the small hill where the shack was, there stood an old woman looking down with a wicked laugh, a short shrill like laugh that scared Little Dink and me to death. We left Zeek and high-tailed it home.

What just happened, I thought as we ran.

As the dark lingered heavier over us, we started to stumble through the woods in our attempt to find our way clear. I could feel the chill bumps on my shoulders, as I expected the witch's hands to grab me any second. I found myself on Spring Street, between Zeek's house and his neighbor's, and I fled home.

The next morning was bright, sunny, and warm. I wanted to call Little Dink and Stump but didn't. I was still scared a little and still couldn't figure out what really happened the night before. There was a knock at our door, I went down and it was Stump, still looking pretty shaken.

Silence. He didn't say a word, and neither did I. We just sat on the front porch swing as we looked off into the distance. What could we say? This was so real and nightmarish. We noticed Little Dink as he walked toward my house. When he arrived he shook his head and sat on the top step. A look of bewilderment was on his face.

"What happened?" I finally asked. "What in the world happened?"

"All I know is that Zeek's mama called my mama a few minutes ago. And my mama said to come get you guys and be over at Zeek's house at ten o'clock this morning," Little Dink said.

"It's about ten now. This doesn't sound good. She's mad at us for trying to scare Zeek. I really don't know if he made it back home or not," I said. "We better get over there before we get into some real trouble."

Little Dink, Stump, and I started to walk slowly out Spring Street toward Zeek's house. We were not in any hurry, but we knew we had to go face his mother. As we rounded Spring Street, we noticed several people already gathered on Zeek's front porch. There was his mother, grandmother, sister, and a couple of neighbors.

"Boy, we are going to get it," Stump said.

Suddenly, everyone on Zeek's porch began to laugh while they pointed their fingers at us. We stopped in our tracks, looked at each other, and moved even slower toward Zeek's house. All of them, including Zeek, were doubled over in laughter.

"It backfired on you, didn't it, Will?" Zeek asked as he tried to compose himself.

As we got closer to the porch there sat the ugliest, oldest, and scariest person I had ever seen in my life. She was dressed in an outfit that would have scared a real witch. We realized we had been set up, the joke was on us, and it worked. Zeek's grandmother, Pearl, was the witch. His mama and grandmother had caught on to what we were up to and quickly put their own plan into action. While we were on the front porch waiting for Stump to get his outfit, sneak back into the woods, and begin his evil attack on Zeek, Granny Pearl slipped out the side door of Zeek's house and went to the shack. We were the ones duped, and it was beautiful. After the explanation we were all in laughter. Part of that laughter was relief because we were no longer in trouble.

Chapter 26
Saved by the Church Steps

It was the middle of June in 1961 or 1962, hot again, and the MilliKids were at my house. We were on the front porch swing like usual, most mornings we stayed out there until we decided what our day's activities were going to be. Little Dink had just told a bad joke (don't remember what it was, usually corny if he told it), but we laughed just the same to make him feel good. Anyway, we were about to head off to the New Holland ball field. Its official name was

Montgomery Ball Park, named after Victor Montgomery, one of the founders of New Holland.

All of a sudden, this car sped around Highland Avenue onto Spring Street. We could hear the wheels as they screeched and saw the car swerve. Then the driver, suddenly and intentionally, drove up onto the sidewalk in front of New Holland Methodist Church. The car rammed the steps and rails. We went to assist. Ordinarily you might see steam as it seared from underneath the car hood but not this time. He wasn't going that fast, he simply couldn't stop.

We didn't know what to expect, but we knew enough to offer help just in case. As we crossed the street, the driver emerged from his door and immediately checked on the occupant in the back seat. A little girl began to cry out of fear, no apparent injury. The mother, we presumed, rushed out of her side of the car and around to the little girl.

"Oh, my God, oh, my God, oh, my God," the mother repeated until she was assured her little girl and her husband were all right.

The husband remained very quiet, probably ashamed or humiliated by what had just happened. Anyway, no one appeared injured.

"The brakes wouldn't work," the husband finally muttered.

"I had no other choice but to run into the steps to make the car stop," he continued to explain.

"Is there anything we can do?" I offered.

"Yes, please, may I use your phone to call my brother for help?" he asked.

"Sure, come on," I said, "and your wife and daughter can sit on our front porch until your brother comes."

It wasn't long before his brother arrived to take them home.

The brother crawled under the car and quickly determined that the brake lines were damaged, which had caused the panic.

"The brakes failed because the line is broken, and there's no brake fluid in it," he said. "Let's go home, and I'll get what's needed to come back and make repairs."

My dad and brother were like that—they could fix just about anything, especially on a car.

I don't remember any police being called or report being made. I don't remember if the church pastor was notified or not. I do know that if Miss Emo, the caretaker of the church, had known, then somebody would have had to pay. Evidently, that didn't happen because the church's rail is still unrepaired today, fifty years later.

The MilliKids had their excitement for the day and something to talk about for weeks to come. It still amazes me, when we talk about that morning how some of the details and circumstances that surrounded the event continue to grow in importance, depending on who tells the story at the time. But it did make for an interesting morning.

A couple of days later we had an awesome summer rain. No lightning, no thunder, just tons of rain, and it was welcomed. The MilliKids enjoyed playing in the rain especially when there was no danger, and this day brought loads of fun. We would lie down in the street next to the curb right in front of Miss Icie's house where Spring Street started going downhill. The rain would rush over our heads and bodies. It was warm, sometimes cool, but always refreshing and fun.

Occasionally, Mr. Paul, an older gentleman who worked in New Holland Cotton Mill, would park his truck between Miss Icie's house and the house next door. Mr. Paul would use the curb to scotch his front wheel, to prevent the truck from rolling down Spring Street. He told us that his battery was dead, and he had to roll it off when he finished his shift at the mill. We understood. He was a kind ole man who loved kids, and we didn't mind him parking on our hill and on our street.

Anyway, this day we lay just in front of his truck, mainly because its presence caused more of a wave of summer rain water to splash onto us and because it was just more fun. We had been there for a few minutes when we decided to take a break and go eat lunch — mothers were calling. As I walked up Spring Street I happened to look down at Mr. Paul's front wheel, where trash and debris had gathered because of the summer rain. A couple of eyes stared up at me. I reached down and there was this doll's head, just the head, nothing more. It was kind of freaky, but I picked it up

Saved by the Church Steps

and took it to my house to clean. Why did I clean it? I have no clue, it just seemed like the right thing to do.

When I cleaned it, I took it to the front porch and put it in one of Mama's pottery vases. I forgot about it. A couple of weeks went by, when one day Little Dink, Stump, and I were out front playing stick ball in the middle of Spring Street. Every now and then we had to take a break when a car decided to interrupt our game. We knew we were okay in the middle of the road and free from Miss Emo's scrutiny.

We noticed that a man had parked on Highland Avenue. He walked up and down as if he had lost something.

"Hey, Will, isn't that the man who wrecked his car on the church steps?" Stump asked.

"I don't know, let's go see," I replied.

As we walked closer, we saw it was him; it was the man who drove the car that morning.

"Hey fellas," he said, "How are you today?"

"Just fine," I said. "What are you looking for?"

"I know you guys remember me from the accident a few weeks back, don't you?" he asked.

We all replied, "Yes, sir."

"Well, that morning before you saw us, I knew we had problems," he continued, "and I also knew I was going to have to do something drastic to get the car stopped. But I was more concerned about my little girl and right about there," he pointed to an area about 100 yards before the stop sign, "I told my daughter to open her door and jump out. Everything would be okay if she did, but she didn't. I wasn't sure what was around the corner, but I figured her injuries would be minimal if she just jumped out before we picked up speed. She couldn't open her door, but instead, rolled the window down and tossed her doll out while she stayed in the car. I didn't know it then, but she told my wife about it a few days later. She hasn't been the same without her doll," his voice somewhat sad and sorrowful.

The MilliKids pitched right in and began to help him look for the doll. At the corner where the two roads met is a drainage area, and Little Dink got down on all fours and begin picking through the rubbish in the drain that had collected through the years. He was sifting through all sorts of trash when he found something. It was the body of the doll, but it had no head. The man said that it was his little girl's. He recognized the body.

Then it occurred to me. Could the doll head I found lodged between Mr. Paul's truck and the street curb possibly be the head that was missing? I quickly ran down the sidewalk to my house, up the steps and retrieved the doll's head from Mama's pottery vase. Even more quickly I ran back up the sidewalk to where the man was and asked him if the head matched the doll. He knew right away, this was the missing head.

"I can't believe it, my little girl is going to be thrilled. You guys will never know how grateful we are. Thanks for everything," his sincerity was evident.

This proud father couldn't wait to get home and share the good news with his wife and little girl. The MilliKids were proud too. Who wouldn't be, helping someone who seemed hopeless?

Chapter 27
Emo's World

Miss Emo was the caretaker of New Holland Methodist Church, one responsibility she took quite seriously. Every MilliKid I know learned how to ride bikes and skate on the sidewalk next to the church and even around the apartment where she lived. It was ideal, the perfect place. But it seemed when certain MilliKids were learning, Miss Emo took exception. She would go out of her way to keep the MilliKids off her sidewalk and away from the church. I had an older brother and sister, Little Dink had an older brother and older sisters, and Stump had an older brother, but they were never chastised by Miss Emo—just us.

There were other MilliKids, long before us, that it would have made sense to keep away from the church and help protect its surroundings. There was a long, long, long list of

MilliKids who were much more mischievous than we were. But, oh no, she had to make our lives miserable, or let me say, try to make our lives miserable, but we didn't let her. As a matter of fact we protected the other neighborhood children from her more than she protected the church from us. You see, we found a loophole, a large loophole, and we took advantage of it.

Miss Emo worked in the mill each weekday from eight o'clock in the morning to four o'clock in the afternoon. During this time we biked, skated, romped, ran, and made the most of the day before she got off work. For a long period of time when people changed shifts in the mill, there was a loud horn that sounded the end of a work shift everyday. It gave us enough warning to leave the church's proximity and continue our fun elsewhere. A couple of years later, the horn was discontinued, which made our trysts around the church a little riskier. Especially around four o'clock, when she got off and began her journey home.

Like I have mentioned many times, MilliKids were never bored. There was always something that would demand our attention or challenge our creativity, and we were creative this day, to a fault. We took an empty half-gallon Sealtest milk carton and cut the bottom out of it. Then we opened the top to form the usual spout and discovered that kite string fed through the bottom and top of this carton made for a lot of fun. We would run twenty to thirty feet of string through it and stand on one end of Miss Icie's porch and let someone hold the other end of the string—almost to the Daniel's house located next to Miss Icie. The inside of the milk carton was coated with wax, which made it very slippery, and we would slide the carton down the string to the person at the other end. The idea came to take it to the upstairs window in my house on the other side of Miss Icie's, and by opening the window we could slide the carton down to her porch.

"Listen everybody," Stump spoke up, "what if we go inside the church steeple and slide the carton all the way down Spring Street?"

We looked at each other, I knew I wasn't going to sneak into the church, climb the ladder all the way to the top, and take a chance on being caught.

"That's it; that's a great idea," Little Dink said. "Count me in."

"Count me out," I responded.

"Me, too," blurted Wart.

So, Little Dink and Stump took the string and carton and entered the church through the side door. The church was never locked. It was a sanctuary, safe and scary, but off they went.

"Do you think they'll go through with it, Will?" asked Wart. "I can't believe they're actually going to do this. They might get hurt or get caught or something."

"No, they'll be okay," I said.

Wart and I sat on my front steps when we heard…

"Will, catch this string when I toss it over," Little Dink bellowed.

"Shhh, shhh, somebody might hear you," I said.

He tossed the spool of kite string over the railing onto the street below.

"Take the string and run to the bottom of the hill," Stump shouted.

Wart and I took off with the spool of kite string unwinding as we went. We reached the bottom of Spring Street and tied it to the old trolley stand.

"Okay guys, it's up to you now," I hollered.

About the time I said it, Stump turned it loose, like a rectangular duck headed for water. It made a muffled screeching sound as it rocketed to the bottom of Spring Street and by the time it ended its journey we were all beside ourselves with laughter. This had never been done. Like I said, we never got bored, and this was worth all the effort and sacrifice, especially Little Dink's and Stump's.

"One more time," Little Dink requested at the top of his lungs.

Wart ran back to the top of Spring Street and through the side door of the church to give it another shot. Again, Wart and I stationed ourselves in front of my house to wait for the second Sealtest shuttle to Cornelia Highway.

"Oh my God, it's Emo!" shouted Little Dink. "Here she comes!"

As he was about to turn the carton loose, he looked down and noticed the mill hands were getting off work. Not quite out of the gate of the mill yet, but her figure was definitely something we had become accustomed to over the years.

"Quick, Wart," I said, "run as fast as you can and untie the string at the bottom of the hill."

About the same time, Stump had removed the carton and dropped the string so he and Little Dink could hurry down.

"There's not enough time." I said, "She will see you. Just find a place to hide in the church and wait until she goes by."

Wart had already loosened the string from the trolley stand and made his way back up to my house through the backyards and terraces that separated the houses from Spring and Carolina Streets. Miss Emo crossed over to the right side of Spring Street, which she did each day and continued to pace herself steadily up the hill.

We couldn't see how close the string was to her, but we knew it was close. Sure enough, about halfway up the hill Miss Emo paused, bent over and picked up the string. She gathered, she rolled, and stuffed it in her purse. She continued — the string seemed endless. We were starting to get a kick out of her puzzlement.

She had to be thinking, *What in the world is this, and where does it end?*

It dawned on her that the string led all the way to the church, and then she finally realized where the end had to be — in the steeple. Stump didn't send it all over the railing. She glanced up, followed it with her eyes, and looked around to see if (perhaps others were watching).

"Oh, my God, those boys. Just wait until I find them," she muttered just loud enough for us to hear her.

This scared us even more, and we dared not move. Wart and I peered through the slotted windows of my bedroom door in the front of my house. She took a turn and hurried up the steps of the church. As the front door opened, Little Dink and Stump almost fell over each other on their way out the side door.

Several minutes passed when suddenly Miss Emo opened the front door and stood there in the doorway full of shock, hands on her hips and lips pursed. We have no clue what she thought because unless she found the carton, she'd never know what went on inside her church that day. She never mentioned one word to any of us MilliKids or our parents, as far as we know.

Several weeks passed by before I had the courage to investigate the milk carton. The bell located in the steeple had not been rung in years because of the unstable platform it was built on. Curiosity got the best of me and one morning, before the village became busy, I crept into the church (quiet, dark, and dreary as it was) and found my way to the steeple's entrance. I slowly climbed the awkward and rickety ladder leading all the way to the steeple floor.

As I made my way through the floor of the steeple, I was breathless, fearful, and yet mesmerized by what I saw. The view of the village was incredible. I looked around, and there was the milk carton. Nestled between the corners of the railing, it was now home to wayward pigeons. They had used the carton for comfort and safety while providing a safe home for their young. Isn't that what a church does?

Chapter 28

Skinny Dip

"Can you guys believe how hot it is today?" Little Dink barked as he ran around the church where we sat.

"Do you think there is a chance we could sneak into Skinny's pool today?" Stump asked.

Little Dink, Stump, Wart, Rusty, and I sat with our backs against the cold bricks on the lower side of the church in the shade. It was the only comfortable place this morning. We tried to stay out of the sun. It was too miserable to play any kind of ball, and no one was in the mood for Monopoly. All we had on our minds was a pool, but where?

None of us had ever been invited to Skinny's pool. Skinny was this huge man, I mean *huge* man, probably six feet or so and well beyond 300 pounds. He lived with his lovely wife on Quarry Street extended, kind of in the city or the "uppity neighborhood" as we called it. He was the biggest man I had ever seen in my life and had this beautiful home and gigantic pool. Skinny was somehow related to my dad. Sometimes he would drop by to say hello, but never stayed long. Anyway, he lived in this beautiful home with an enormous pool. We would often ride our bikes over to his house just to see it. Something to dream about.

"You know if we entered his backyard through the pasture area I bet he couldn't see us," Rusty suggested as he swatted the gnats and wiped the sweat from his forehead.

"Yeah, if we hike past the Boy Scout Cabin, we might be able to take a dip," I said.

The local Boy Scouts troop had built a cabin located in the woods adjacent to Skinny's property. We had never ventured that far, and it didn't sound like a good idea today. The heat stifled us, and we sweltered with no relief in sight. Skinny's was not close by, and none of us wanted to hike through the woods to get there. We'd dug a swimming hole in my backyard only last summer, but that didn't work. When we dug a pretty big hole and turned on the water, the ground just sucked it up. Before you knew it, we had to fill the hole back up with dirt.

"I've got an idea," I said, "but it's going to take some help from you guys and a neighbor to make it work. "Let's sneak through the window of the gym to the pool area and see if it's possible for us to fill it up with hoses from outside spigots."

We weren't sure if the pool would even hold water, but we were desperate, and right now this sounded like a great idea. From where we sat next to the church, we could actually see the window that would hopefully ease us from this sweaty misery. Even though it was during the middle of the day, we crept ever so gently to the loosened window in the pool area of the gym. We quickly slid through it and onto the deck that surrounded the pool. After we surveyed our possibilities, we decided this might be worth the effort.

"Stump, get your hose. Wart, go get yours, and Little Dink go get…"

"I can't. My Dad will kill me if I drag that thing off down here," he said. "There's no easy way for me to get ours without him seeing me. Wait a minute," Little Dink said. "Even if we do get all these hoses hooked up, do you actually think we will be able to fill the pool today?"

"You're right. I didn't think about that. It will take forever to fill that pool up," I said. "But, if we start today, maybe we can enjoy it in a few days."

Everybody scattered, doing his best to make this a more enjoyable summer. We found three outside spigots at our disposal and hooked up the hoses we had gathered together to reach the pool. Stump had three different hoses and connected them to his spigot. We were able to put three more together and connect them with Miss Bee's (the unknowing neighbor) spigot. She lived next door to Stump and probably would have given us permission if we had asked, but we didn't. Finally, two hoses were connected to the spigot just outside the gym. We fed them through the empty pane of glass of the pool windows and into the pool itself.

Before we turned the spigots on, we made sure the drain at the deep end of the pool was completely covered so there would be no wasted water when we started. We would have to test it anyway, but we felt confident it would hold.

"Turn them on," I hollered, "and let's see what we got."

The gym had been condemned for several years. Local government officials said it was a fire hazard and decided to shut it down, but we still played basketball, fox-and-hounds, and other games in it when we could. We always felt a little skittish about being in the gym because it was supposed to be off limits. It was our sanctuary at times. This was one of those times. The water flowed.

"It's filling, it's holding, it's not leaking," Little Dink said, "I believe we did it. Let's go and forget about it for a while."

"This is going to be terrific," Wart bellowed, "I can't wait."

"Do you know how to swim, Wart?" I asked. "Aren't you afraid of the water?"

"You don't worry about me, Will," he replied.

I don't remember what we did for the next two days, but we did check on it from time to time to make sure the water was still in full flow, and it was. It's funny, the grownups never said a word to us (I imagine because the water cost only two dollars a month regardless of how much was used). Anyway, paradise was about to become real. We even invited some of our other buddies to come join us.

Our little adventure began on a Friday afternoon and by two o'clock Sunday we had almost a full pool, enough for us to take a plunge. Most of the MilliKids went to church, so we agreed to meet afterwards. We brought our swim trunks to the gym to change there.

"Who's first?" I asked. I knew I didn't want to be. The water was pretty clear, you could actually see the bottom of the pool.

Stump didn't waste a second before he jumped.

"Yeow, wooh, wee," he screamed.

"Oh my gosh, oh my gosh," Little Dink shouted as he took the plunge, "this is *freezing!*"

He came out quicker than he went in. But before you knew it, all of us were wet. We yelled from all the excitement and the cold water. We couldn't talk because our teeth chattered. It was, indeed, the coldest water any of us had ever been in, but before too long we became accustomed to it. Our first contest was to see who would be the first to bail, and of course it was Wart. The longer we stayed the better we felt. We swam and moved around constantly to help ease the freeze.

Two of our buddies couldn't swim, but they stayed in the shallow end and had fun just the same. It was a memorable day for all of us. We discovered that the pool could still hold water, but, without the steam boiler to keep the water warm, the temperature was frigid. We enjoyed the pool for two more days before it drained.

Sometime Wednesday afternoon, I went to check on the pool. We had removed all the hoses except the one from the spigot near the gym. We figured maybe one hose would be enough to help us keep enough water in the pool. After further investigation, we discovered that a neighbor had caught on to our mission and removed the remaining hose. I believe Stump got into trouble with his parents, but he never said anything, and we didn't ask. His dad helped serve as the gym attendant occasionally, and I'm sure he was wise to us, but chose not to spoil our fun for a couple of days.

Why do adults have to spoil everything? We were just a bunch of kids looking for a cold place to play on a hot summer afternoon. We created one, if only for a short time, but we did have a ball that summer week. We never made it to Skinny's pool, and we never invited him to ours.

Chapter 29
The Fire

Millhouses were made out of pine. Even walls and ceilings were tongue and groove. Why so many more of these duplex homes never caught on fire is beyond comprehension. Maybe they were just that well built, who knows, but we had a few catch fire during my childhood. Not one of them burned to the ground. Probably because of how well they were built and our volunteer fire department, who eventually helped save the day. You can still visit the village today and see the ground floor of the three homes that burned. One home was up the street from where I lived. The Wilkes lived there, and one night the MilliKids helped save their home and possibly their lives.

Another warm, balmy, summer evening in the 1960s, and we had an awesome round of fox-and-hounds in process. The predetermined play area was the two blocks from Myrtle Drive to Carolina Street. Little Dink, Wart, Rusty, and Burney were on one team while Stump, Zeek, Root, and I were on the other. We were the Foxes for this round and had hunkered in our hiding places. Root was a new kid to the crew. Born late in life to a much older mother and father, we instantly became his siblings in a way. He was short with wild blond hair, a smart-mouth, and an agitating personality — especially when he knew someone was around to protect him, and I was usually the one who protected him. Anyway, we hid behind the old church in some shrubs. We noticed that the Hounds had gone in a different direction in hopes of finding us, so we could talk and whisper a little until they sniffed us out. We sniffed first. It was quite unusual; we smelled something on fire. As we looked around we noticed the Wilkes' home had smoke that billowed from under the roof line.

"Look, hey, look everybody, at the smoke around Smug's house," I announced loudly.

Smug Wilkes was an older MilliKid who lived in the house with his disabled mother. Quickly, all of us started running toward Smug's house. We hammered on the front door with our fists and alerted Smug and his mother about the danger. The Hounds caught on and joined us as well. Smug ran upstairs and immediately discovered something was terribly wrong. By that time the New Holland Volunteer Fire Department had been called, and we could hear the siren alerting the neighbors and firemen. People from every direction began to pour in near the house that was ablaze.

"Will, help me get Mama out of here," Smug insisted. "She uses a cane and can't move very fast."

The Fire

"Come on, Miss Jack, let's go outside where you'll be safe," I urged.

"What's going on? What's the matter, boys, what are you doing?" she pleaded.

"Miss Jack, we think your house is on fire, and you need to get out," I begged.

"No, no, no, please God, no, not our home," Miss Jack pled.

"Smug, what are you doing? Get out of there! We can hear the fire engine on its way," Little Dink yelled.

"Come here, Little Dink, and help me with this refrigerator," Smug asked.

"You're crazy. Get out of this house! You might get hurt or die," Stump shouted.

Smug was trying to save what appliances he could. The fire engine had arrived and, after being assured that all the people were out of the house, Mr. Rudy, the volunteer fire chief for the night, began directing the other firefighters on the plan of attack. Men in their masks and fireproof suits with hoses on their shoulders were already on the roof. The MilliKids had all gathered on the lawn across the street from the Wilkes' home.

"Why are you crying Root?" I asked. "Everyone is safe and outside."

Root was young and had never been around this much excitement. Now that I think of it, none of us had ever been around this much either.

"Come on, men," Mr. Dyer urged. "Help me with some of this furniture. We need to save what we can."

The firemen tried to save whatever they could to minimize the Wilkes' loss. The refrigerator, TV, and other small items were safely removed. It was an amazing sight, firemen on the roof, going through both upstairs windows trying to extinguish the flames that ravaged the home. What effort! Something I had never witnessed before. It seemed like in no time they had the fire under control and eventually snuffed.

"Okay men, it's under control, come on out and let's establish a controlled perimeter," Mr. Rudy ordered.

He positioned firemen all around the house to keep watch for any flames that might reignite. Most of the community was present, and many of the men and women made sure Miss Jack and Smug had a place to stay and food to eat. I wasn't sure where they would settle for the evening, but I did know the village was a family that night.

For the next few days, the refrigerator and other items that were spared remained on the front lawn. One day Little Dink, Stump, and I noticed that Smug and his mother were at the house, so we offered to put the items on the porch if we could.

"Hey, Smug, need any help in moving your fridge and all," I asked.

"Yeah, they're pretty heavy, but I've got a hand truck, and if you'll help me, we'll put them on the front porch," he said. "By the way, thanks for your help the other night. We

The Fire

didn't know anything was going on until you guys came to the door."

"You spoiled our fox-and-hounds game, you know?" I snickered.

"If you guys had not been outside playing, who knows what might have happened," he said. "Anyway, Mama's much better, and I think we will have this place fixed up in a couple of weeks. Daddy already has some men coming to make repairs. We can't live with his brother's family long. We've started to get on each other's nerves now."

To watch the repairs on the Wilkes' home was another event to remember. They were able to save the main floor, but they had to remove the top floor. So much progress was made in just a couple of days that we knew Smug and his mama would soon return to their new home. Actually, when it was finished, it appeared to be in much better condition than it was before the fire.

Mr. Speck, Smug's dad, didn't live with them at the time, and I can only speculate why, but he was on the scene of the restoration from day one. He personally made sure that Smug and his mama had a place they could still call home. At one time, Mr. Speck coached a local baseball team, and if memory serves me correctly, a very good one at that.

"Boys, I just want to thank you again for your alertness and quick reactions the night of the fire," he began. "This is my family. We are having our problems, but one day maybe we'll all be together again. Anyway, thanks."

What if we hadn't increased our area of play that night? What if we decided not to even get up a game at all? Yes, the MilliKids were kind of a gang, a crew, but even more so, we were a bunch of kids who cared. The fire probably even brought us closer together, but more importantly, I believe, it made us more aware of our neighborhood.

I'm not sure if the Wilkes ever became a family again, but they certainly have to remember that living in New Holland was special. Smug and I actually worked in the mill together before we both joined the Navy. He and I were never close friends, but we understood one thing quite well—every person has a purpose. You may not know where or when you are needed most, but when that time arrives be ready to answer the call. As far as I know, Smug spent most of his life as a career officer in the Navy. He offered his life in defense of our country and for millions he didn't know, but he took an oath to die for one and all.

The Volunteer Fire Department stayed in force for several years afterward and, yes, they had to answer other calls. They saved other homes, and without any fatalities. As a matter of fact, I don't recall any firemen being injured. It appeared they operated under oath as well. To save, protect, and defend what we so proudly call the Village of New Holland, Georgia. Later on, the county fire department would serve New Holland and the surrounding areas and our own fire department had to close its doors. It served its purpose and so did its men.

This petition to restore the gym in New Holland, was one of our last acts as MilliKids.

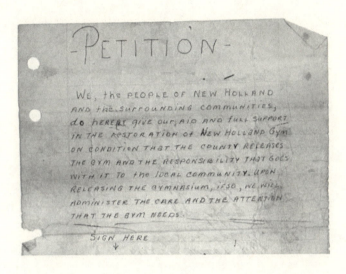

Governor Lester Maddox's response to our petition.

Executive Department
Atlanta

Lester Maddox
GOVERNOR

Thomas T. Irvin
EXECUTIVE SECRETARY

July 2, 1968

Mr. Vic Wilson
5 Spring Street
New Holland, Georgia 30501

Dear Mr. Wilson:

May I take this opportunity to thank you for your letter of June 26 concerning the gymnasium in Hall County.

I am most appreciative of the confidence you have placed in me and assure you that I, too, am very interested in the youth of our state and nation. Through recreation, young people receive an opportunity to participate in competitive sports and various other wholesome activities. Also, a program of this type is a better preventer of juvenile delinquency than any other available.

You stated in your letter that this gym belongs to the Hall County Board of Education. Therefore, I am taking the liberty of contacting Mr. Herbert L. Strickland, Superintendent of Schools, Hall County, and informing him of your desire to have this facility made available to the local community group.

May I suggest that you have adult citizens of New Holland to organize and make an application to the Hall County Board of Education so they might be in a position to assure school officials that they are willing and capable of opening and maintaining this facility for community use.

With kindest regards and best wishes, I am

Sincerely,

Lester Maddox
Governor